PRAISE FOR THIS BOOK

"Titus 2 is one of my favorite passages in all the Bible. Now we have a wonderful guide to walk alongside us as we study and digest this incredibly important text for the church today. Sarah and Matt have written a book that is biblically faithful and practically rich. It is so very well done. I will be quick to commend it to others who want to grow and mature into the likeness of our Savior."

—Danny Akin

President, Southeastern Baptist Theological Seminary

"There's nothing quite like making simple things in life cumbersome. Sometimes that happens with books on discipleship; they come across as though you've got to have a theological degree, maybe an extra certificate in counseling, and take it on as a part-time job. But Matt and Sarah Rogers in *From Generation to Generation: Fulfilling the Great Commission One Life at a Time*, explain how discipling others is within reach for anyone walking with the Lord. Instead of overcomplicating the process, they help readers see how daily life patterns can turn into discipling opportunities. I'm going to encourage our community groups to get this book, read it together, and see how each believer can help others who aren't quite as far along the journey as they are. This book will encourage Christians to be involved in discipleship!"

—Phil A. Newton
Retired Pastor; Pillar Network Staff; Author

"Evangelism and disciple-making must never be separated, because true salvation always leads to sanctification. In a world of increasing disconnection, the Rogers call Christians back to the glorious and gritty work of personal, life-on-life discipleship. This task is not reserved for pastors or spiritual "rockstars"—it belongs to every believer. Matt and Sarah are trusted guides who write with humor, candor, and biblical faithfulness. For those who have never discipled anyone, this book is an excellent place to start. And if you long to see a culture of disciple-making grow in your church, read this book carefully and give several copies away."

—Aaron and Deana Menikoff
Pastor and Pastor's Wife, Mt. Vernon Baptist Church

"From Generation to Generation is a timely and essential resource for churches hungry to recapture

the heart of discipleship. Matt and Sarah Rogers present a compelling, biblically grounded vision for life-on-life investment—rooted in Titus 2—that moves disciple-making out of the theoretical and into the relational rhythms of everyday church life.

This book dismantles the modern myths of discipleship as a program or platform and restores it to its rightful place as a Spirit-empowered, person-to-person calling for every believer. With a sound biblical perspective, relatable stories, and practical instruction, the Rogers offer a clear path for cultivating a culture where older believers invest in the next generation with gospel intentionality.

Accessible, pastoral, and deeply needed, *From Generation to Generation* is more than a manual—it's a movement back to God's design for multiplying mature disciples in the local church. Every pastor, ministry leader, and church member will benefit from this vision."

—R. Scott Pace, Ph.D.
Provost, Dean of Graduate Studies,
Jim Shaddix Chair of Expository Preaching,
Professor of Preaching and Pastoral Ministry

"'You cannot give what you do not possess.' This quote from one of my seminary professors encompasses the heart of Matt and Sarah's book. We are all called to the essential work of investing in the next generation, but that means we have to be disciples ourselves to make disciples. In *From Generation to Generation*, Matt pours out of the reality that he and Sarah have lived through years of life-on-life discipleship in the local church. We are most powerful and compelling as disciplers when we engage the risen Savior and receive the salvation and life change He offers.

The biblical framework Matt provides showcases the gospel's power to transform lives through generations, and he invites all of us to get in the game of being disciples and making disciples. I will be recommending this book to our staff and others for a long time."

—Matt Williams
Pastor, Grace Church, Greenville, SC

"As a Christian, Jesus's plan for your life is to be a disciple-maker. Regretfully, for a variety of reasons many of us feel ill-equipped. In *From Generation to Generation* Matt and Sarah Rogers offer us an inspiring, empowering, and practical toolbox for becoming everyday disciple-makers. Their humility is inviting. Their experience is assuring. Their transparency is refreshing. Here, every Christian reader finds clear biblical foundations, simple next steps, and helpful guiding principles for a lifetime of disciple-making in the home, in the church, and in the everyday rhythms of life."

—Tony Wolfe

Executive Director-Treasurer,
South Carolina Baptist Convention

FROM GENERATION

TO GENERATION

FROM
GENERATION
TO GENERATION

Fulfilling the
Great Commission
One Life at a Time

MATT & SARAH
ROGERS

For the generations who will come after us...
may they be found faithful.

From Generation to Generation:
Fulfilling the Great Commission One Life at a Time
© 2025 Matt Rogers and Sarah Rogers

ISBN 978-1-955295-67-3

Cover Design: Rachel Rosales
Typesetting: Rachel Rosales
Editing: Lauren Spano

COURIER PUBLISHING

100 Manly Street
Greenville, South Carolina 29601

Printed In the United States of America

TABLE OF CONTENTS

Foreword   i

Introduction   v

1. From Person to Person   1
    Titus 2:1

2. From Older to Younger   31
    Titus 2:2-3

3. From Heart to Mouth   55
    Titus 2:2-3

4. From Example to Practice   73
    Titus 2:4-6

5. From Once in a While to All of the Time   95
    Titus 2:7

6. From Distant to Disciple   111
    Titus 2:8

7. From Theory to Practice   135

8. From One to Many   157

Conclusion   187

Appendix 1: Discipleship Resources   191

Appendix 2: The 7 Arrows of Bible Reading   195

FOREWORD

If you've been a Christian for any length of time, you understand that the church's mission is to make disciples. The clarity of this mission is stated in Matthew 28:18-20, the Great Commission. The centrality of this mission is revealed in the record of the ministry of the apostles in the book of Acts. They preached the Word. The early Christians devoted themselves to their teachings. Then they lived life together, helping one another become more like Jesus (Acts 2:42-47).

Sadly, this is not what many churches experience today. We are witnessing the fruit of rising individualism, suspicion of authority, and a growing aversion to organized religion. In response, pastors and church leaders have tried various approaches. The seeker-sensitive movement sought to draw Baby Boomers back to church. Later, the emergent church tried to recapture Generation X. But strategies tailored to one generation often fail to carry over to the next. We need a more enduring approach, one that transcends generational trends.

Matt and Sarah Rogers believe we already have that approach in the example of Jesus and the apostles. Christ has structured his church to fulfill this mission by giving ministers of the Word to equip the saints for disciple-making (Ephesians 4:11). The foundation of this work is the Word of God. That's why the early church was devoted to the apostles' teaching. But as James reminds us, hearing the Word isn't enough; we must also do it. As the Word is preached, the church is called to speak it in love to one another until we all reach maturity in Christ (Ephesians 4:12-16).

Now, if all this book did was call us back to this biblical model, it would be worth reading. But the Rogers do more. They help us understand what it means to be a disciple and how to make disciples in our own day. They root their vision in Paul's instructions in Titus 2 and offer practical counsel for how that might take shape in our churches and homes.

If we want to reach the next generation, we must return to the ways of Jesus and his apostles.

Matt and Sarah show us how. With two decades of pastoral ministry and a life lived together in the local church, they are not speaking as distant theorists. They model what they write.

So read this book. Reflect on it. Discuss it with others. Pray through it. Then go make disciples of all generations.

Juan and Jeanine Sanchez
Austin, Texas 2025

INTRODUCTION

Imagine your life without technology. Even the most technologically averse among us recognize that the world is powered by technology. Here we're speaking primarily of digital technology—texts, emails, WhatsApp messages, Alexa, Google, Instacart, Grubhub. We use digital technology so frequently that we fail to quantify the way our lives are powered by these tools.

But the world hasn't always run on technology, at least not the digital kind that's ubiquitous today. In a long-ago land there existed people whose primary means of interfacing with the world wasn't through a little screen they kept in their pocket.

Actually, that land existed not so long ago, and there's still a generation alive that fondly remembers such a world. The previous world was present, local, and relational.[1] Your engagement in the world was largely limited to the community in which you resided. Apart from newspapers or travelers, your knowledge of the world was derived from the places you lived, learned, worked, and played—and you did all of those in the same locale.

Everybody's favorite, *The Andy Griffith Show*, memorialized the fictional town of Mayberry—a quaint Southern town with stories, drama, romance, dynamite-eating goats, and endearing characters like Barny, Otis, Helen, Thelma Lou, Floyd, Goober, Gomer, and good ole Ernest T. Bass. What made Mayberry endearing was the simplicity of it all. Today's world feels a long way from Mayberry.

The local church, particularly the church in the United States, feels these changes. The early forms of church were deeply woven into the fabric of a specific location. Look at most American cities today and you'll find a First Baptist Church or First Methodist or First Presbyterian at the city's center. Life happened in a small geographical cir-

---

1. Wendell Berry captures the essence and value of place for one's identity and rootedness. For example, see *Jayber Crow* (Berkeley: Counterpoint Publishers, 2001). There are also entire volumes reflecting on the theme of "place" throughout the redemptive story such as Craig G. Bartholomew, *Where Mortals Dwell: A Christian View of Place for Today* (Grand Rapids: Baker, 2011).

cle, and those who lived in that circle knew one another. They met and interacted, not just when the church gathered on Sundays, but daily as their paths crossed.

Modern transportation afforded the option for people to move to the 'burbs. The suburban sprawl in America isolated people from one another. Now people often live in one place, work or study in another, and, in many cases, are members of a local church in yet another place. People's lives are divided, as are their relationships.

Add technology to this mix and you have a toxic combination. Now, people do not even have to be physically present to work or learn or shop. They can do all that with the swipe of a finger from the comfort of the couch. Human interaction can be completely removed.[2]

Times have changed. We've adapted and adjusted to these new, technological toys, and they've

---

2. The impact of digital technology on modern society is a popular theme in current writing. For a popular level treatment consider Samuel James, *Digital Liturgies: Rediscovering Christian Wisdom in an Online Age* (Wheaton: Crossway, 2023). An advanced, academic work that is marvelously written and worthy of the work required to read it well is Antón Barba-Kay, *A Web of Our Own Making: The Nature of Digital Formation* (Cambridge: Cambridge University Press, 2023).

become a way of life for most.[3] But the fact that we've adapted does not mean these changes have been for the better.[4] The friction that once fostered real relationships is now gone and, as we will argue in this book, the loss of real relationships lies at the core of the anemic discipleship seen in many churches today.

It's not just technology that's changed the church, though technology has certainly altered the way many do ministry.[5] Technology is but one ex-

---

3. This is not to suggest that it is wise to put our head in the sand and not recognize the dangers digital technology poses to our world, our families, our churches, and our very selves. For a robust treatment of the challenges brought about by a technologically powered world consider L. M. Sarcasas, *The Analog City and The Digital City* https://www.thenewatlantis.com/publications/the-analog-city-and-the-digital-city or a more readily accessible volume like Tony Reinke and John Piper, *12 Ways Your Phone is Changing You* (Wheaton: Crossway, 2017). Also note Trevin Wax's article regarding the impending challenges of AI: "AI and the Threat of Mutually Assured Boredom" https://www.thegospelcoalition.org/blogs/trevin-wax/ai-threat-boredom/.

4. This point is made in popular books which posit that the causes of many social ills in our day can be traced to the death-grip technology has on most. For example, Jonathan Haidt's work, *The Anxious Generation: How the Great Rewiring of Childhood is Causing an Epidemic of Mental Illness* (New York: Penguin Press, 2024).

5. Here we need only to think about the advent of video venue preaching, online "church campuses," "online pastors," or social media publicity to notice the ways that digital technology has changed the way many do church. A robust critique of these mod-

ample of a tool that would rightly be described as "trellis" in the now common contrast put forward by Colin Marshall and Tony Payne in their excellent book, *The Trellis and the Vine*.[6] They question whether the church has grown so enamored with the work of building the trellis—the various structures and programs of the church—that it has lost sight of the vine—the work to disciple people to maturity in Christ (Eph. 4:11-16). They argue that the real work of ministry is what happens with the vine. The vine work is where true discipleship takes place and the trellis is meant to support the growth of the vine, not the other way around.

It might be helpful to think of a food pyramid, which provides a simple visual of what types and amounts of food a person should consume in a healthy diet. You have fruits and veggies near the bottom, with meat just above, and sugary desserts

---

els of ministry is beyond the scope of the current work, though it is worth questioning whether these so-called advances in the way the church operates are doing more to promote healthy church life or are actually depleting such vitality. For a critique of these models see Jonathan Leeman, *There's No Such Thing as Virtual Church* https://www.thegospelcoalition.org/article/no-virtual-church/.

6. See Colin Marshall and Tony Payne, *The Trellis and the Vine* (Sidney: Matthias, 2009).

at the top. Were we to trace a healthy discipleship pyramid, it might look something like this:

Healthy Discipleship Pyramid

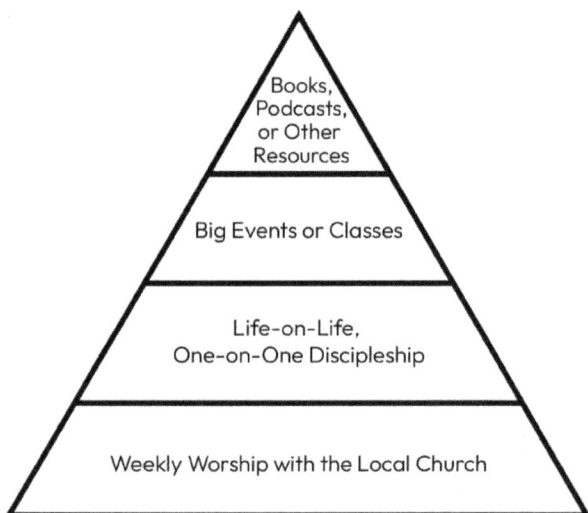

Books, Podcasts, or Other Resources

Big Events or Classes

Life-on-Life, One-on-One Discipleship

Weekly Worship with the Local Church

You'll notice that the base of the pyramid is the weekly gathering of the saints on the Lord's day in the local church. We believe God created His church to be the life-blood of the people of God. There people should be fed through a steady diet of faithful, expositional preaching that clearly and compellingly communicates the truth of Scripture. The Word is also sung through gospel-rich songs that testify to the truth of Jesus' work. God's people offer prayers to God that affirm a robust under-standing of who God is and what He is doing in the world. These steady, weekly means of grace are to be the regular diet of the people of God and the primary means by which discipleship is fueled.

The next step up the pyramid is the work we are arguing for in this book—the life-on-life, one-on-one ongoing work of a Christian to walk with another person as he or she grows into Christ-like-ness.[7] Then, in the context of weekly worship and life-on-life discipleship we add in appropriate classes, seminars, or events that provide specific instruction in core doctrines and practices of the faith. Finally, we supplement our diet with digital technology and books that aid our discipleship and devotion.

Sadly, this healthy discipleship pyramid is of-ten rearranged.

---

7. In his book, *The Word-Centered Church: How Scripture Brings Life and Growth to God's People*, (Chicago: Moody, 2017) Jon-athan Leeman speaks of the Word preached from the pulpit re-verberating like electricity from a power plant as Word-centered Christians take the proclaimed Word and minister it to one anoth-er in one-on-one conversations, small groups, or classes.

Common Discipleship Pyramid

Life-on-Life, One-on-One Discipleship

Weekly Worship with the Local Church

Big Events or Classes

Books, Podcasts, or Other Resources

Many believers start with resources—books, blogs, podcasts, sermons—from those outside of their church. They feast on technology. Maybe they love a certain author or preacher and tend to consume everything that person produces. Or they depend on technological algorithms to suggest resources they might like. In our day such content is easy to find and simple to stream. While these digital resources may be tasty, their role in the discipleship diet plan is the equivalent of building your daily calorie intake on macaroni and cheese and banana puddin'.

From there, many move to big events or classes, either led by their church or some other ministry or organization. Churches plan conferences or send people from the church off to an event, hoping that all of the effort will pay off and the conference will produce radical change. Or we think that the various training venues offered at our church—our Sunday classes or small groups—will be able to do the heavy lifting of discipleship. We're not suggesting that events or programs of the church are inherently bad. Nor are we saying that disciples cannot be formed in these venues. We are saying, however, that they are insufficient to form the foundation of one's discipleship diet.

I (Matt) have been a pastor for almost two decades. I've sat in counseling sessions with people navigating almost every complex situation under the sun. I've prayed with people enslaved in sin and rebellion. Many of these people wanted to change—all needed to change. My experience suggests there is one factor that differentiates those who do change from those who don't, and it has little to do with any trellis the church might provide. The key factor is almost always the life-on-life investment of another person. For change to happen, people need someone else in the church who walks with them, encourages them, helps them, prays with them, reminds them of the truth of God's Word, and does this over and over again until the struggling individual finds freedom and peace.

Let's say that on a particular night there's a small group meeting at the church, and one man shares that he's struggling with anger and resentment towards his wife. That alone is a miracle. Most often, people merely acknowledge the surface-level issues they are facing—busyness at work, a health scare, or some concern with a child. It's rare for people to share their sin. But, in this man's case, the Spirit of God did a unique work and he humbled himself to share and ask for prayer.

What next? How does such a man change?

Theologically, we would rightly say that such a man changes by the power of the Spirit of God bringing conviction and repentance that produces lasting fruit (Rom. 12:1-2; 2 Cor. 7:9-13). Yes! But practically, how does movement happen? Most of the time it happens when another man in that group hears this man share, approaches him after the meeting, exchanges phone numbers, and offers to meet up for lunch. The second man doesn't stop there. He continues to text the man Scripture to encourage him, calls to ask how he is doing, and holds him accountable in this area. Over time, as the relationship deepens, the second man is privy to various patterns of thought or action that indicate anger in the man's heart, and he may call him out when he sees him making small compromises. Little by little, the man changes through the simple power of a friend who invested and cared.

The same pattern holds true when you ask people to reflect on their spiritual journey. As a pastor, I get the joy of talking to people who want to join our church. In those membership meetings, I ask them about how God saved them and how they grew in their faith. Occasionally the person will mention a sermon, sometimes a conference or a church. But most often it's Joe or Frank or Ruth or Alana—the names of people who took an interest in them—often at a key time in their lives—and discipled them toward maturity in Christ. Many times, the people mentioned didn't even know they were discipling the person; they would have likely just thought of it as being a friend. But God used these personal relationships to be a conduit of grace and a help toward transformation.

As a pastor's wife and a mother with a new-born and toddler at home, I (Sarah) benefitted from older women who not only served our family by bringing meals and helping clean my house, but who also prayed for me and pointed me to Jesus for daily provisions of grace. The transition from one to two children was the most difficult for me, especially since my own mom passed away when I was a sophomore in college. Women from our church served as spiritual mothers in my life to teach me how to love my husband and children, work as unto the Lord, and pursue godly character through it all.

Our guess is that every reader of this book can look back in the rearview mirror of life and notice the same pattern. The older you get, the more likely you notice the significance of these relationships in shaping you as a follower of Jesus. And this is no accident. ***The primary argument of this book is that life-on-life discipleship is an essential means of grace that God uses to sanctify His people in His church.***

In the pages that follow we will seek to prove this point and show you how the Bible provides a roadmap that empowers all Christians to give their lives to this critical work. Using Paul's letter to Titus,[8] we will see the not-so-secret sauce for transformation—both of an individual's life and of entire churches.

---

8. Throughout the book we will use the Christian Standard Bible as our normative Bible translation.

CHAPTER 1

FROM PERSON
TO PERSON

"But you are to proclaim things
consistent with sound teaching."
Titus 2:1

There's a certain stretch of river in western North Carolina that I (Matt) know by heart. It's more than merely knowing the name of the river or being able to point it out on a map. I know the rocks, the turns, and most importantly, the pools where hungry trout like to feed. There are other rivers in the area that I don't know, but I know this one.

Why?

This river has been *my* river since I was old enough to fish. Obviously it's not actually *my* river. It's a heavily trafficked public river right off the main road. But it feels like my river because of my dad. He grew up in the area and fished those same rocks as a child. Later in life, he and my mom made it a family tradition to head back to that same stretch of river where my dad taught me how to fish. Sporting my extra-small waders and a Zebco rod and reel combo, I'd set out with my dad and fish the river. Along the way, he'd teach me about how trout feed and how best to present the bait to entice them to bite. Perhaps more importantly, he taught me how to stand up on the slick rocks and manage the flies, the lures, the rod, the net and everything else that was necessary to be successful on the water. In time, I found my stride, and by my teen years I could catch fish in that stretch of water with my eyes closed, often when no one else around was catching anything. Dad taught me to fish and he taught me to love fishing. Because of his investment, that river became my river.

Everyone has examples like this. It might be hunting, or golf, or cooking, or cheering on your favorite sports team. Something got in our bones because someone older than us loved that thing and taught us to love it too.

For me (Sarah) it's music. My parents loved to sing and our home was filled with music. The lyrics of the great oldies—Elvis, The Beach Boys, The Supremes—alongside gospel groups and hymns are imprinted in my memory. In the car, my dad and mom harmonized with "I've Got You Babe" by Sonny and Cher while my sister and I hummed along in the backseat. We followed them into small churches across the outskirts of Columbia, South Carolina as they sang with their gospel group, The Branches. My sister and I even joined them on stage a time or two. My parents gave me my first record player as a young teenager and I listened for hours to the musical strains of The Beatles, America, and Simon and Garfunkel. When I was a kid, my dad chose the hymns and led worship for our church, and I followed in his footsteps by leading worship for our youth group through my high school years. I still serve on our church's worship team today. Immersing our home in music provided opportunities to exercise my voice, taught me the joy of sharing music with others, and showed me the power and beauty that music can evoke.

Herein lies the argument we want to make in this book. While it's certainly true that all relationships matter, **perhaps the most important relationships are those between older and younger Christians.**

The Apostle Paul's letters provide a glimpse into God's relational design for his church. Three of those letters—the Pastoral Epistles—are written to Timothy, who pastored in Ephesus (1 and 2 Timothy), and to Titus, who pastored in Crete. Because Timothy and Titus were pastors, these letters bring ecclesiology front and center. They are meant to provide guidance for topics such as what the church is, how the church should be led, and how the church should live out its mission in the world.[1]

---

[1]. Among the best commentaries on the Pastoral Epistles are R. Kent Hughes and Bryan Chapell, *1-2 Timothy and Titus: To Guard the Deposit* (Wheaton: Crossway, 2012); Gordon D. Fee, *1 & 2 Timothy, Titus* (San Francisco: Harper & Row, 1984); Donald Guthrie, *The Pastoral Epistles.* Tyndale New Testament Commentary. 2nd ed. (Grand Rapids: Eerdmans, 2007); Thomas Lea, *1, 2 Timothy, Titus.* New American Commentary. (Nashville: B&H, 1992); William D. Mounce, *Pastoral Epistles* (Word Biblical Commentary. Nashville: Thomas Nelson, 2000); David Platt, Daniel L. Akin, and Tony Merida, *Exalting Jesus in 1 & 2 Timothy and Titus* (Christ-Centered Exposition Commentary. Nashville: Holman Reference, 2013); Philip G. Ryken, *1 Timothy* (Reformed Expository Commentary. Phillipsburg: P&R, 2007); John R. W. Stott, *The Message of 2 Timothy: Guard the Gospel* (The Bible Speaks Today, Downers Grove: InterVarsity Press, 1999).

So it is no surprise that 1 Timothy and Titus contain many of the same themes and arguments.[2] A primary focus in both letters is the church's leadership. In Titus 1:5-9 and 1 Timothy 3:1-7, Paul outlines the qualifications for an elder/pastor in the church.[3] Pastors should be men of character, calling, and competence so they can do the work of shepherding God's people (see also 1 Peter 5:1-5).

---

2. These two letters roughly parallel the correspondence between Ephesians and Colossians. Since the context and time of writing is similar the content and argument is similar in both letters. In terms of 1 Timothy and Titus the main differences likely relate to the fact that Paul served and ministered in Ephesus for three years and the church was more established in that location, whereas Titus' work in Crete was at an earlier stage of development. Also Paul's seemingly closer connection with Timothy prompted more personal commentary in the letters and caused Paul to write Timothy one additional letter (2 Timothy) just before his death.

3. It is beyond the purview of this book to make an apologetic for church polity. The case for plural elder leadership has been made clearly and compellingly in numerous volumes including Mark Dever, *Nine Marks of a Healthy Church* (Wheaton: Crossway, 2000); David Dickson: *The Elder and His Work* (Phillipsburg: P&R Publishing, 2004); Derek J. Prime & Alistair Begg, *On Being a Pastor: Understanding our Calling and Work* (Chicago: Moody, 2004); Phil A. Newton, *Elders in Congregational Life: Rediscovering the Biblical Model for Church Leadership* (Grand Rapids: Kregel, 2005); Phil A. Newton: *40 Questions about Pastoral Ministry* (Grand Rapids: Kregel, 2021); Mark Dever, *The Church: The Gospel Made Visible* (Nashville: B&H Academic, 2012).

In his letter to Titus, Paul then transitions from the discussion of pastoral ministry into the work of local church members. It's not merely pastors who have an assignment to the people, but the people have a role to play in building up the church as well. Paul begins chapter 2 of Titus this way:

> But you are to proclaim things consistent with sound teaching. Older men are to be self-controlled, worthy of respect, sensible, and sound in faith, love, and endurance. In the same way, older women are to be reverent in behavior, not slanderers, not slaves to excessive drinking. They are to teach what is good, so that they may encourage the young women to love their husbands and to love their children, to be self-controlled, pure, workers at home, kind, and in submission to their husbands, so that God's word will not be slandered. In the same way, encourage the young men to be self-controlled in everything. Make yourself an example of good works with integrity and dignity in your teaching. Your message is to be sound beyond reproach, so that any opponent will be ashamed, because he doesn't have anything bad to say about us (v. 1-8).

This paragraph is the focus of the remainder of this book. This paragraph is all about relationships and the way that life-on-life ministry promotes the spiritual health of God's people in God's church.

On the surface, the instructions are fairly straight-forward, but it seems that much of the lackadaisical nature of discipleship in the church derives from a failure to apply Paul's counsel here. In more succinct fashion, Paul makes the same point in his final letter to Timothy: "What you have heard from me in the presence of many witnesses, commit to faithful men who will be able to teach others also" (2 Tim. 2:2). Paul intends for one generation to pass along the "faith that was delivered to the saints once for all" (Jude 3).

A CREATION PATTERN

Long before the birth of the New Testament church (Acts 2), God created the world with a mechanism for multiplication. The first couple was given the mandate to "be fruitful, multiply, fill the earth, and subdue it" (Gen. 1:28). Adam and Eve bore the divine imprint, the *imago Dei*. Had they been faithful, the entire cosmos would be increasingly filled with people who image God and worship Him rightly."

God created embodied souls (Gen. 1:26-28).[4] Flesh and blood, soul and spirit, all intermingle in what makes a person human (Gen. 2:7). Try as we might, it's impossible to fully separate these various elements of humanity. There may be a time and place, such as in a theological discussion about biblical anthropology, where differentiating between the flesh, the mind, the soul, the spirit, and the heart may be helpful. But such nuance can easily undermine the fundamental reality that God packaged all of that into a singular person. So what happens to the body impacts the soul, what influences the heart comes out of the mouth, and what shapes the mind empowers action with our hands and feet. We should not be surprised that the flesh-and-blood in-

---

4. It is hard to overstate the importance of Genesis 1:26-28 in shaping our understanding of God's mission in the world. In these few verses, we are introduced to God's mission to fill the earth with His glory and do so through people who represent Him as His image bearers. Among the books that have most influenced my understanding of the mission of God and the image of God from Genesis 1 and 2 are Stephen G. Dempster, *Dominion and Dynasty: A Theology of the Hebrew Bible* (Downers Grove: Inter-Varsity Press, 2003); Craig G. Bartholomew and Michael W. Goheen, *The Drama of Scripture: Finding Our Place in the Biblical Story* (Grand Rapids: Baker, 2004); Albert M. Wolters, *Creation Regained: Biblical Basics for a Reformational Worldview* (Grand Rapids: Eerdmans, 2005); Edmund P. Clowney, *The Unfolding Mystery: Discovering Christ in the Old Testament* (Phillipsburg: P&R, 1988).

teractions with other people have an impact on our heart and soul.

Of course, this mission would necessitate biological reproduction. Adam and Eve would have children who would bear God's image and reflect His character throughout the world. However, the task of biological reproduction created a pattern that would extend far beyond child-bearing.

Sin entered the world, and with it the task of multiplication grew far more complex. Now, humans multiplied sin and not God's perfect image. Broken image-bearers filled the earth with other broken image-bearers who misrepresented God's character in their rebellion (Rom. 1:18-32). All those in Adam's line bear this mark of depravity (Rom. 5:12), as seen vividly in the murderous rage of his first child, Cain (Gen. 4), and the monument to self-importance at Babel (Gen. 11).

The reality of sin doesn't mean that the task of multiplication is rendered obsolete, however. Even after God judged His creation with the flood, He once again reinstated the creation task by telling those preserved in Noah's flood to "Be fruitful and multiply and fill the earth" (Gen. 9:1). In other words, the work of filling the earth with image-bearing worshipers is still in effect, even on the other side of sin. Like all work, however, the task of multiplication is now fraught with difficult thorns and thistles (Gen. 3:18).

AN OLD TESTAMENT ROADMAP

The entire Bible makes clear that God made people for relationships.[5] "It is not good for man to be alone" (Gen. 2:18) is a stark claim for God to make in a world that up to that point is only good and very good (see Gen. 1). God saw a relational void and provided for the first man. This provision extends far beyond the bounds of marriage. Though relationships easily go off the rails (see Gen. 4), human interaction is built into God's created order. He works through families (Gen. 12) and nations (Ex. 19) to work out His plan of redemption. Since people are relational beings, we should also not be

---

5. Consider Bruce Milne, *We Belong Together: The Meaning of Fellowship* (Downers Grove: InterVarsity Press, 1978). This simple book provides a biblical grounding for the necessity of human relationships in the Chrisitan life. See also James C. Wilhoit, *Spiritual Formation as if the Church Mattered: Growing in Christ Through Community* (Grand Rapids: Baker, 2008). Wilhoit takes the popular spiritual disciplines, such as Bible reading and prayer, and shows that they are not intended to be isolated, privatized disciplines, but are rooted in the community of the local church and reach their maximum potency when they are applied within the context of genuine relationships.

surprised that God will use these very relationships to accomplish His good work in our lives.

This multiplication mandate continued through the nation of Israel, which was given instructions regarding how they were to fulfill God's mission in spite of the brokenness of sin. The call to transmit the faith to the next generation shows up in, arguably, the most significant section of the Pentateuch, the Shema. There the Lord gives instructions for his people when they enter the Promised Land. Moses charges them:

> Listen, Israel: The LORD our God, the LORD is one. Love the LORD your God with all your heart, with all your soul, and with all your strength. These words that I am giving you today are to be in your heart. Repeat them to your children. Talk about them when you sit in your house and when you walk along the road, when you lie down and when you get up. Bind them as a sign on your hand and let them be a symbol on your forehead. Write them on the doorposts of your house and on your city gates (Deut. 6:4-9).

The call is simple and clear—Love the Lord alone and love him with all that you are. No surprise there. God's design for His image bearers is, and has always been that they would reflect His glory and love Him whole-heartedly (Gen. 1:26-28). What might be surprising is that right there in this famous passage we find the method for transmitting this love for God. Love for God and obedience to God were meant to be transferred from one generation to the next.

God's covenant people, the nation of Israel, would transmit this faith primarily along the lines of the biological family. Parents would commend God's virtues to their children. They warned about the folly of idolatry. They pointed their children to God and taught them to love Him wholeheartedly. And they modeled sole devotion in such a way that their children would be compelled to love and follow God by virtue of their parent's example. They would do this all the time and everywhere, not merely in the places and activities that were commonly thought of as sacred acts of worship. To this point, Christopher Wright comments:

The priests of Israel were, indeed, to teach the law, but not as something only they within the confines of the professional guild could understand. On the contrary, the law was to be the topic of ordinary conversation in ordinary homes in ordinary life, from breakfast to bedtime.[6]

The devolution of Israel in the book of Judges is evidence of the failure of the nation to do just that. The people unravel and do what is right in their own eyes as one generation repents and returns to the Lord, only to see the next capitulate to folly (Judg. 17:6). The neglect of the work of multiplication likely resulted in the maddening refrain in the Old Testament history books (1 and 2 Samuel,1 and 2 Kings, 1 and 2 Chronicles). We meet one king who loves God, follows Him, and destroys the false idols of His day. Then comes his son, who doesn't love God, placates idols, and faces judgement (see 2 Kings 22). Israel cannot faithfully obey God, so they certainly cannot consistently transmit the faith from one generation to the next.

---

6. Christopher Wright, *New International Biblical Commentary: Deuteronomy* (Peabody: Hendrickson Publishers, 1996), 100.

JESUS' EXAMPLE

Jesus himself picks up on this multiplication mandate, doing in His ministry what Israel's leaders could not. Jesus, the very Son of God, did not go about His earthly mission alone. He chose 12 disciples—men with whom He would share His life for three years (Mk. 3:13-19; Lk. 6:12-16). Jesus entrusted His work to these disciples, urging them to feed the hungry crowds (Matt. 14:13-21) or cast the demon out of the tormented man (Matt. 17:14-21). He then sent the disciples and other followers out into the neighboring towns and villages to proclaim the gospel and to heal the sick (Lk. 10:1-12).

In his masterful treatment on the subject, Robert Coleman suggests that "Jesus' plan was to enlist men who could bear witness to his life and carry on his work after he returned to the Father."[7] Two points are important here. First, Jesus could have done the work himself but He intentionally modeled multiplication. And, Jesus could have focused on the multitudes, but instead He concentrated His efforts on a few.

Coleman poignantly applies Jesus' method to subsequent disciples:

---

7. Robert E. Coleman, *The Master Plan of Evangelism* (Grand Rapids: Revell, 1993).

It will be slow, tedious, painful, and probably unnoticed by people at first, but the end result will be glorious, even if we don't live to see it. Seen this way, though, it becomes a big decision in the ministry. We must decide where we want our ministry to count—in the momentary applause of popular recognition or in the reproduction of our lives in a few chosen people who will carry on our work after we have gone. Really it is a question of which generation we are living for.[8]

Such an assignment is at the heart of Jesus' famous Great Commission found in Matthew 28:18-20. Throughout His earthly ministry, Jesus has echoed the call of the Shema: "Love the LORD your God with all your heart, with all your soul, and with all your mind. This is the greatest and most important command" (Matt. 22:37-38). Faith in Jesus' work and the indwelling power of the Spirit of God would make it possible for sinners to love God in this way. Those who love God are then commissioned to "Go, therefore, and make disciples of all nations, baptizing them in the name of the Fa-

8. Ibid., 35.

ther and of the Son and of the Holy Spirit, teaching them to observe everything I have commanded you" (Matt. 28:19-20). This mission provided the marching orders for the first disciples and extends to all Christians throughout history who are to give themselves to the work of multiplying disciples of Jesus Christ, especially making disciples of future generations of Christians.

In our day, it's easy to needlessly divide the work of evangelism and disciple-making in the church. Often the thought is that evangelism is something we do prior to someone coming to faith in Jesus and discipleship something that happens next. Such a contrast is largely unnecessary, since the work is connected in Jesus' assignment. We are commanded to go, share the gospel, see people come to faith and subsequently be baptized, and then teach those people how to love and follow Jesus through the local church. Since there is often an anemic level of discipleship among the church, it may well be that we are investing in life-on-life discipleship with someone who's come to faith years ago and has simply not been taught how to follow Jesus. Sometimes, we will have the joy of seeing someone come to faith and walking with that same person as they grow and change. Either way, we are representing our King as we call others to love and follow Him.

THE NEW COVENANT CHURCH

Among the church, the new covenant people of God, such generational transmission would transcend the bounds of one's family of origin (Eph. 2:11-22, 4:11–16). This is not to suggest that parents should not play a central role in the spiritual formation of their children akin to what we read in Deuteronomy 6. However, it is to suggest that the context for transmitting the faith from generation to generation extends to those united in God's new family and brought together through the blood of Christ (Eph. 2:11-22). In the church, Christians are to pass on the faith to subsequent generations.[9]

---

9. Now, these arguments are not new. Theologians have consistently noted the relational orientation of God's mission. One such example is the Christian classic by Dietrich Bonhoeffer, *Life Together: The Classic Exploration of Christian Community* (New York: Harper Collins, 2009). For my money, Bruce Milne's, *We Belong Together* (Lisle: InterVarsity Press, 1978) is the best treatment of the subject; however, the fact that this book is largely out of print now means it may require a bit more of your money than you care to invest. Another option is Joseph Hellerman's *When Church was Family: Recapturing Jesus' Vision for Authentic Christian Community* (Grand Rapids: B&H, 2009). Unfortunately Hellerman's foundational argument in the book is often overshadowed by some of his application, which seems a bit too communal for the average

We will use the word "disciple" and "discipleship" as shorthand to refer to this multigenerational, one-on-one, life-on-life model that we are advocating for in this book. **A Christian disciple is a person who is saved by grace through faith in Jesus Christ and is being transformed by the Spirit to reflect God's glory in every area of life.**

Notice the verbs in that sentence—salvation and transformation are accomplished from a source outside of the person, namely, through God's work on our behalf. After receiving salvation by grace through faith, disciples then "follow in Jesus's steps, doing as Jesus taught and lived."[10] A Christian can, and will, grow, but God ordains to produce this growth through relationships in the church. Discipleship is simply helping someone love and follow Jesus Christ through His church.

---

reader from an individualistic, Western society. I'll leave it to you to decide what you make of that critique, but the book is still a wonderful treatment of the community God intends for His church.

10. Mark Dever, *Discipling: How to Help Others Follow Jesus* (Wheaton: Crossway, 2016), 13. Dever's book in the Building Healthy Churches series is a master-class on disciple-making. Much of what we intend to do in the present volume is to apply Dever's overview of disciple-making to the local church through the lens of Titus 2.

The Apostle Paul emphasizes this life-on-life investment in 2 Corinthians 5:17-21:

> Therefore, if anyone is in Christ, he is a new creation; the old has passed away, and see, the new has come! Everything is from God, who has reconciled us to himself through Christ and has given us the ministry of reconciliation. That is, in Christ, God was reconciling the world to himself, not counting their trespasses against them, and he has committed the message of reconciliation to us. Therefore, we are ambassadors for Christ, since God is making his appeal through us. We plead on Christ's behalf, "Be reconciled to God." He made the one who did not know sin to be sin for us, so that in him we might become the righteousness of God.

It's imperative that we notice that God entrusts all those who have been reconciled to Himself through the work of Jesus with this glorious message of reconciliation. God does not reserve the work of being an ambassador, or a disciple-maker, for superstar Christians. The work is not merely for those who've arrived at some predetermined level of maturity. Rather, He entrusts the message of reconciliation to all believers who work on His behalf to implore others to be reconciled to God and to embrace all that comes to those who are now given a righteous standing before God. This is how God has always worked.

This point may be obvious, but consider the fact that an omnipotent God could do what He wants any time and in any way He chooses. He doesn't need humans to do His bidding. He didn't need Adam in order to come up with the names for the animals. Nor did he need Moses to go to Pharaoh in order to get the Israelites out of Egypt. This point is undeniable when one considers the supernatural nature of the plagues and the miracle of the Red Sea deliverance. A God who can do all that surely doesn't need a stammering, fearful person to do His bidding. But God chooses to work through ordinary people to accomplish His superordinary purposes in the world. After the ascension of the Lord Jesus and the sending of the Spirit, God intends the outworking of His work in the world to take place through the local church (Eph. 3:8-13).[11]

---

11. For a robust definition of the local church see the following classic works on the subject: John S. Hammett, *Biblical Foundations*

God can, and does, use interactions between Christians in various churches to aid in our growth. For example, you might bump into a believer at the supermarket and have an edifying conversation. Or you might call an old friend who lives in another part of the world and find hope and help in a difficult moment. But we are suggesting that the ordinary means of relational grace that God gives to his people should take place within the context of a local church, where people have covenanted together to worship and obey Jesus. Together, this new family acts in dozens of ways to grow into the full measure of Christ-likeness (Eph. 4:11-16).[12]

---

for Baptist Churches: A Contemporary Ecclesiology (2nd ed.; Grand Rapids: Kregel Academics, 2019); Mark Dever, *Nine Marks of a Healthy Church* (4th ed.; Wheaton: Crossway, 2021); Mark Dever and Jamie Dunlop, *The Compelling Community: Where God's Power Makes a Church Attractive* (Wheaton: Crossway, 2015); Conrad Mbewe, *Foundations for the Flock: Truths About the Church for All the Saints* (Hannibal: Granted Ministries Press, 2011); Richard D. Phillips, Philip G. Ryken, Mark E. Dever, *The Church: One, Holy, Catholic, and Apostolic* (Phillipsburg: P&R, 2004).

12. We will certainly mention many of these aspects of the New Testament church's life together as we progress in this book. However, commentators commonly refer to these traits as the "one another" commands for Christians in the church because many of the exhortations follow this paradigm. For example, "love one another" or "serve one another" or "bear one another's burdens." The lists vary, but there are over 30 one another commands in the New Testament in passages like John 13:34; Romans 12:10, 16;

Discipleship aids all Christians in embracing their new life in Christ.

Susan Hunt, the former director of women's ministries for the Presbyterian Church in America, coined the term "spiritual mothering." In her book of the same title, Hunt argues that in the New Covenant, men and women who've been adopted into God's family have the responsibility to pass down sound doctrine as spiritual fathers and mothers to the younger generations of the church.[13] This term helps to shape the way we view our fellow members and our role in the church. Church members do not join a club where we wave to each other as we participate in our shared hobby. Instead, we join a family which needs mothers and fathers, sisters and

---

15:5-7; Colossians 3:16; 1 Corinthians 12:25; Galatians 6:2 and Hebrews 10:24 among many others.

[13]. See Susan Hunt, *Spiritual Mothering: The Titus 2 Model for Women Mentoring Women* (Wheaton: Crossway, 2016). Hunt's emphasis parallels the theme of our thesis here, however, the language of mothering highlights the necessity of this work starting in the home. Mothering isn't merely something the church does, but it is primarily something mothers do in relationship with their children. Life-on-life discipleship is meant to take place in the home as parents are faithful to nurture the hearts of their children and train them in accordance with God's word (Ps. 127; Prov. 22:6). We will return to this theme in a later chapter and describe the way intentional parenting paves the way for local church disciple-making.

brothers to sharpen our faith. And while we joyfully affirm godly male leadership in the church, women's roles are elevated in the life of the church by Paul's exhortations that they are to learn and then to teach younger women what is good. The Bible is clear from cover to cover—people help other people love and follow Jesus.

Before going further, it's worth pausing to consider why a resurgence in life-on-life discipleship is needed in our day. First, many people, including many Christians, are lonely. People are more isolated than ever and seem to be awakening to the deadly implications of their lack of community.[14] Jonathan Haidt's recently published work, *The Anxious Generation*, connects the rise of digital technology and the modern epidemic of mental health issues, especially among today's teens.[15] Of note for the

---

14. Robert Putnam's *Bowling Alone: The Collapse and Revival of American Community* (New York: Simon and Schuster, 2020) captures the essence of the ever-increasing individualism that pervades American life. Putnam doesn't write as a Christian, but as a sociologist who laments the decline of communal life and begins to trace the implications of such trends, many of which we are seeing worked out in our world today some 25 years after the book was first published.

15. See Jonathan Haidt, *The Anxious Generation: How the Great Rewiring of Childhood is Causing an Epidemic of Mental Illness* (New York: Penguin Press, 2024). Haidt and his colleagues have writ-

present discussion is the way technology isolates. Rather than enjoying real relationships in time and space, people are left with curated relationships over pixels and screens. What is perhaps encouraging about this seemingly universal reality is that the misery of anxiety and depression may drive people to seek alternative solutions. If the malaise of digital pseudo-community falls flat, the church is poised to enter that void and present an alternative community comprised of actual relationships.

Also, there seems to be a bounce-back effect from the jarring isolation brought about by the Covid-19 pandemic. Life changed, seemingly overnight. Gone were backyard cookouts, birthday parties, even weddings and funerals. Days turned to weeks, which turned to months. Depending on your location, the restrictions regarding social distance lingered for years. While people continued to function, social distance could not become a way of life for communal image-bearers. People experienced the practical, social, and psychological implications of their isolation. Now, several years

---

ten extensively on this subject in numerous scholarly and popular articles, such as Jonathan Haidt and Jean Twenge, "This is Our Chance to Pull Teenagers out of the Smartphone Trap" https://www.nytimes.com/2021/07/31/opinion/smartphone-iphone-social-media-isolation.html.

removed from the peak of the crisis, people seem to be longing for the relationships they missed and those they learned they needed, more than perhaps they thought before Covid hit.[16] Again, the church is given a chance to thrive. Where better for those who want human connection to find genuine relationships than in the church?

Next, many Christians, including those who should now be making disciples, have never been discipled themselves. I've preached approximately 1,500 sermons over the last 20 years. Among those are dozens that address the subject of disciple-making and these sermons are often met by a chorus of "amens." Frankly, it's not difficult to prove from Scripture that Christians should be about the work of making disciples.

But then let's say you have a 22-year-old man come to faith in Jesus. He's baptized and, like most new Christians, demonstrates zeal to learn and grow. Take that young man and introduce him to an older man in his 60s who's been a church member for decades and say something like, *"I'd love*

---

16. For example, See Sara Zeff Geber at Forbes who writes on the need for in-person relationships in the broader culture in her article, "It's Time for Three Dimensional Relationships Again" https://www.forbes.com/sites/sarazeffgeber/2023/02/11/its-time-for-three-dimensional-relationships-again/.

for you to spend the next year with this young man to teach Him to love and follow Jesus." Your request is a functional restatement of the Great Commission. Far too often, however, your request would likely be met by fear or insecurity that this old saint doesn't really know how to obey the Great Commission. He wants to. He "amens" sermons about the Commission, but he's not equipped to do the work.

Some are fortunate to grow up in homes where the gospel was taught and lived out by believing parents, but such generational disciple-making in the home is far from the norm. In an ideal world, the means to learn how an older disciple invested in younger men and women with gospel intentionality would be wired in us from our upbringing. This is what we would have experienced our parents do for us each day.

Our church is composed of many younger members and, while some came from the homes of believing parents, even many of these members lament the lack of disciple-making that took place in their homes. More often than not, young Christians either come from families of those who do not love and follow Jesus, or from homes where the gospel was assumed and the responsibility for disciple-making was abdicated to the church.

Since most Christians haven't had disciple-making multiplication modeled in the home, they depend on the church and her pastors to create a pathway for them to learn how to make disciples and multiply their spiritual lives without the benefit of modeling in the home.

This brings us to another reason a disciple-making resurgence is needed. Often, pastors struggle to actually equip people to make disciples. Pastors have limited bandwidth, and the task of equipping the church takes time, so busyness in other good activities can divert attention from this primary task. If the pastors aren't careful, the demands of ministry programs and plans can overwhelm their calendar and attention. Many times, pastors themselves have never been discipled, so they are seeking to create a culture that they've merely read about but not experienced. Even those who have been discipled often fail to invest the time, energy, and strategy it takes to create a multiplication culture.

Pastors who disciple will start by investing in the work personally. They take a couple of young men and begin the work to invest in them and then encourage them to do the same for others. Multiplied over years and lives, the flywheel of disciple-making can start spinning and multiplication can become normative. But it takes time for this to happen.[17]

There are also changes within church culture that make this a prime moment for a renewed focus on life-on-life discipleship. The American church in the 80s and 90s was captivated by the allure of church growth. Bigger and better was the name of the game. Megachurches became common, along with sprawling facilities, bloated staffs, buffet-like programs, and ever-increasing Sunday attendance numbers.[18] As churches grew, so did the complex-

---

17. There are many factors that may impede a discipleship culture from taking root in the church, but a faithful pastoral team must be diligent to invest in the work and not merely blame circumstantial factors for a lack of disciple-making in their congregation. Many would suggest that the chief fruit of the ministry of Capitol Hill Baptist Church and 9Marks will not be the vast amount of books and resources they've created through the years, as helpful as those have been, but the people who have been discipled by pastors like Mark Dever. See Dever's book *Discipling: How to Help Others Follow Jesus* (Wheaton: Crossway, 2016) or the testimony of now-faithful pastors who've been heavily influenced by Mark's attention to one-on-one discipleship through the years. See a summary from one such brother here: https://ftc.co/resource-library/articles/nine-ways-ive-seen-mark-dever-disciple-men-and-raise-up-leaders/.

18. Many have voiced criticisms of the church growth movement and the underlying pragmatism and consumerism that tended to define churches during this era. An early spokesman was David Wells who wrote extensively on the subject in *No Place for Truth: Or Whatever Happened to Evangelical Theology* (Grand Rapids: Ee-

ity of fostering life-on-life relationships among the masses. Large churches were (are) not the problem. People can hide in a small church or a big church. Churches of all sizes are grappling with solutions to address the spiritual health of their congregation. Every year, evangelical conferences offer sessions entitled "How to Build a Discipleship Culture," books are written on the subject, consultants are hired to create scalable models for disciple-making, and church staff spend hours discussing how to leverage their existing programs to facilitate life-on-life ministry. There's much good that results. What's dangerous is that far too often we, as church leaders, approach these resources as if they are going to offer a silver bullet to fix a stagnant church culture. Plug and play, or so we think. But such quick fixes— whether models or programs or strategies—fall flat and we are right back at the drawing board trying to reinvent our systems one more time.

Thankfully, we think there is an answer. It's not a quick fix or simple strategy. You are still going to have to pray and plod for years before you see

---

rdmans, 1994) and *Above All Earthly Pow'rs: Christ in a Postmodern World* (Grand Rapids: Eerdmans, 2005). The point here isn't to critique the megachurch, but to highlight how the challenges of this model of being the church present opportunities for new ways of connecting God's people in the church.

the flywheel start to spin. But we think it's possible to create vibrant, life-on-life relationships in the church where people help other people follow Jesus.

Even more, we believe that robust intentionality to facilitate a culture of life-on-life discipleship will foster the health of local churches far beyond what any program or event or conference can accomplish. Relationships are God's design for disciple-making. In much the same way that digital technology can replace the beauty and simplicity of real people in a real place in real relationships, so too can the programs and ministries and services and missions and budgets and buildings supplant the main work of the ministry that is meant to take place in our local churches. We want to challenge you—whether you are a pastor or a church member—to give yourself wholeheartedly to God's design for discipleship in the local church through intentional relationships. But these are not just any relationships. We need a certain kind of relationship—one that Paul makes clear in the section that follows in Titus 2.

CHAPTER 2

FROM OLDER
TO YOUNGER

"Older men are to be self-controlled, worthy of re-
spect, sensible, and sound in faith, love, and endur-
ance. In the same way, older women are to be reverent
in behavior, not slanderers, not slaves to excessive
drinking. They are to teach what is good."
Titus 2:2-3

We've attended hundreds of small groups through
the years. Not all were called small groups, but the
premise is the same—a dozen or so Christians meeting together to study the Bible, pray, talk about life,
bear burdens, and build community. Some of the

sweetest moments of Christian community happen in these smaller settings.

There's a danger, however.

Many of these groups are composed of people who are all basically the same. I don't mean they are the same in the sense that their preferences and personalities are the same. You've always got some people who like True Crime podcasts, others who prefer The Great Indoors, some who overtalk and some who barely talk at all. Get a few people together and you'll surely have these types of differences. That's not the rub. What's challenging is that these groups are often composed of people who are at virtually the same age and stage in life.

Here's how it goes.

The topic of conversation for that night is around Hebrews 13:5 and the warning to avoid the love of money and to live content in the present moment. One young husband in the group admits this is a struggle for him and asks how he can pursue contentment when he's early in his career and feels pressure to advance so he can provide for his wife and family. He wonders aloud what form contentment takes at this life stage. Another describes the intense pressure she feels about money because she's got over a hundred thousand dollars of student loan debt. She doesn't feel like she loves money, but she's far from content because of the massive hole she's dug for herself. She asks the group how to be content.

Crickets.

No one knows how to respond other than the vague, theoretical concepts that they've heard other people say through the years. *"On their deathbed, no one looks back on their life and wishes they'd worked more,"* someone says. *"Have you thought about changing jobs?"* another asks. *"I think I know a guy who's hiring in your field. I'll set up a conversation for you."* And so it goes. None of this is bad, but it hardly goes far enough to provide actual help. What these fictitious small group members need most is another Christian who is a step or two in front of them in life who can provide guidance, point to Scripture, and testify to God's faithfulness in the face of financial fear.

THE DANGER OF SAMES

Donald McGavran is often referred to as the father of the church growth movement. Writing in the 70s and 80s, McGavran famously posited that people come to Christ most effectively and efficiently if they do not have to cross ethnic, racial, social, or generational barriers to get there.[1] If this premise is true, he argued, churches would be wise to create communities of homogeneous people, those who have as much in common as possible. In so doing, these homogeneous groups can attract, evangelize, and disciple other people like them. Other churches, composed of a different homogeneous subset, can do the same for that demographic and so on. No need to create diverse, multiethnic, or multigenerational communities because people feel most comfortable when they are around a bunch of people just like them.

Many have challenged the homogeneous unit principle, and with it the church growth movement as a whole. They argue that such pervasive pragmatism undermines God's activity in saving sinners and places undue burden on man-centered techniques to build the church.

Instead, the diversity of the local church both racially, socially, and generationally is a foretaste of our heavenly reality (Rev. 5). This isn't to suggest that every church must be maximally diverse, but it is to press against the assumption that homogeneity is ideal. God unites diverse people into the church

---

[1.] Donald A. McGavran, *Understanding Church Growth* (Grand Rapids: Eerdmans, 1970), 190-211.

who share little in common apart from faith in Christ and the indwelling of the Spirit (Eph. 2:11-22; 4:5-6).

While many would argue against homogeneous churches, there is still a temptation to structure church ministries according to common social and generational divisions. Perhaps the most common example is the age-graded division of many Sunday School classes and Bible studies where you have a class for young professionals, another for those 35-45, still another for those 45-55, and on and on. The larger the church, the smaller the age categories in order to account for class size.

On the surface, it makes sense to organize church life in this fashion. After all, people who have recently retired share much more in common with other retirees than they do with those on the front end of their careers. Empty-nester families are so far removed from dirty diapers and temper tantrums that it's seemingly wise to keep these groups separated. As the logic goes, let's use these smaller groups to connect like-minded people and then they can unite with the broader subset of the church during weekly worship. Such logic is compelling, but it rarely works that way. Most of the time, once these groups form, they tend to move as a pack through the rest of church life, forming deep relationships with one another and having limited connection with those outside of their homogeneous community.

A less common but even more problematic model happens when the church creates groups on the basis of shared affinity. Again, the motive seems honorable. Create a small group for those who ride motorcycles, those who enjoy working out, or moms who homeschool their kids. Not only are there built-in connections, but it's likely easier for those in these subgroups to connect throughout the week. However honorable the motive may be, the latent pragmatism shows through since the rationale is to do what seemingly works. The short-term wins of age-graded or affinity-connected groups may undermine the most significant power source the church has to produce disciples who last.

DID YOU SAY THAT WORD?

Paul's instructions to Titus are built around one type of person, but it's a category most of us don't like to think about. His challenge focuses on older men and older women: "**Older men** are to be self-controlled, worthy of respect, sensible, and sound in faith, love, and endurance. In the same way, **older women** are to be reverent in behavior, not slanderers, not slaves to excessive drinking. They are to teach what is good…" (Titus 2:2-3).

The adjective "older" provides an immediate hindrance to most heeding the exhortation of this passage. Simply put, no one likes to think of themselves as "older." We tend to reserve that category for people who are two life stages in front of us, only to passively resign ourselves to being "older" when there isn't anyone alive two life stages in front of us. When a pastor exhorts the older members of the church, it's as if everyone is looking around the room like he's talking to someone else.

At the time of writing, I (Matt) am 46 and Sarah is 42.[2] My wife answered a question in a small group discussion and passively said something like, "*I'm the oldest woman here tonight so…*" I looked around stunned. Surely not! But she was right. And if she was the oldest woman in the room then what was I? Not only were we the oldest people in the group, but we had a good decade on most everyone else there. Mid-40s isn't old, is it? For the purposes of Paul's instructions to Titus, 40 is plenty old enough to get to work.

---

2. Don't tell her that I told you her age since you aren't supposed to mention a lady's age in public, much less in print.

There are a number of ways we should think about this older demographic in the church. First, "older" should refer to people who are considered older in the culture based on their age. Of course the line of demarcation will shift from culture to culture, but those at retirement age in the US (approximately 65 and up) are older, like it or not. While it is certainly true that chronological age does not always equate to spiritual maturity, church members who are chronologically older in the culture should heed the instructions given in this text.

Next, the age of the church will have something to say about who is older. I (Matt) pastor a church that is young. We aren't as young as we once were, but especially in the church planting stage of the church's life it seemed like everyone was 26 years old, married for three years, and pregnant with their first child. We've since aged, and the church has diversified, and for that we are grateful. But we are still a young church. A 40-year-old man in our church is an older man; whereas, that same man may not be perceived as old in a different church composed of more senior saints.

Also, spiritual maturity plays a role. This comment is dangerous because many will use it as an excuse and suggest that they must cross some threshold of sanctification in order to qualify to do what Paul tells older Christians in Titus 2. "Yes, I'm old," some may say, "but I'm still immature in my faith, and I've got so much to clean up in my life first." Such a response speaks to the posture of our hearts. Rather than asking, "How can I position myself to obey this passage?" we often ask, "What can I do to avoid having to do what the text demands?" A perceived lack of spiritual maturity should not be used as a *Get Out of Responsibility Free* card. But spiritual maturity does play a role in this conversation.

Maturity acts as a multiplier on our age. Someone who is 50 but who came to faith within the last year after being passively connected to an anemic church for decades is likely not as "old" as is a 30-year-old who came to faith in her teens, was discipled by her parents, and grew in faith in the context of a healthy church. To provide some objective metric, anyone who has been a Christian for over a decade and can point to evidence of growing Christian character should consider themselves qualified to play the role of "older" in this passage. If not, this lack of maturity and obedience should be considered a sin issue for which the person must repent. They are acting as babies in Christ, when they should be growing in maturity and helping others walk with Jesus (1 Cor. 3:1-2; Heb. 5:11-14).

This brings us to the final way to understand who is old. If you've been a Christian for more than a decade, then you are likely "older" than some other Christian in your church. So a college student is an older man to a middle schooler. A young mom is an older woman to a college freshman. A middle-aged couple is older than the couple just returning from their honeymoon. This isn't to suggest that merely existing as a Christian qualifies you to act as an older man or older woman, but it should suggest that everyone can do something. Even if you aren't chronologically older, you can engage as an older person in the life of someone in order to get some experience in the work of disciple-making as you age.

I said that was the final way to think about "old," but there's a bonus. One other significant type of older person in the church is the pastor.

THE PASTOR(S) AS AN OLDER MAN

The term "pastor" is used synonymously with the term "elder" (see Acts 20:17-38; 1 Pet. 5:1-5). The role of elder was common in the ancient Near East in all forms of society. An elder was an older member of the community who was a de facto leader on the basis of his accumulated wisdom, maturity, and experience. Applied to the church, elders are appointed on the basis of their character and competence for the work of shepherding God's people (1 Tim. 3:1-7; Titus 1:5-9). Though it is not a biblical requirement that a man be a certain age in order to pastor, the use of the term "elder" should caution us against appointing younger men for the work. If a younger man is appointed to pastor, he should be uniquely distinguished as a man whose spiritual maturity significantly multiplies his chronological age.

This means that the first reference to an older man in Titus is a call to Titus himself. In verse 1 Paul says, "You proclaim things consistent with sound teaching," and the "you" there is Titus. In other words, the lead domino to create a discipleship culture is the pastor acting as an older man and calling other older men and older women into the work. This parallels what Paul says is the fundamental task of church leaders. They exist "to equip the saints for the work of ministry, to build up the body of Christ" (Eph. 4:12). The pastor, as an older man himself, is to start the process by teaching things consistent with sound doctrine. This includes, at least in part, teaching the character traits that older men and women are to embody listed in verses 2 and 3. The pastor is then given the task of doing the things he asks older men to do as he serves as an example to the flock.

It's easy for pastors to excuse themselves out of this work. Few would suggest that they do not bear the responsibility to make disciples, but most either explicitly or implicitly believe that their disciple-making activity is exclusively done through public preaching and teaching or through their work to lead the church. We want to affirm the formative role that pastors play in shaping disciple culture in these ways. Sadly, it's become common among some camps to devalue preaching specifically, or even the role of vocational pastoral ministry as a whole. Often those writing such critiques press against the hierarchical models of pastoral ministry that isolate a pastor from the congregation or create a hierarchical structure that suggests that some pastors are of a different class of Christians than is the average member of the church. Drive-by sermons divorced from genuine pastoral care are deadly. But we need not devalue the role of sermons or the pulpit in order to suggest that pastors should also be invested in one-on-one relationships where they practice disciple-making on a personal level. It is possible to do both.

Pastors also invest in the work by directly challenging older men and women to engage in the work of disciple-making. The link is clear between verse 1 and verses 2 and 3 in Titus 2. "You (pastors) are to commend these things to older men and older women," Paul says. Here again, it is not enough for pastors merely to challenge older men and women from the pulpit, such as when they preach sermons on passages like Titus 2. This is good, but it's not enough. Pastors should also do three things. First, they should disciple a few men themselves. Next, they should directly meet with older saints in the church and encourage them to engage in the work of disciple-making. These "have you thought about" conversations are often a means to stir the souls of those sitting on the sidelines.[3] Finally, pastors should find small gatherings of older saints in the church where they can exhort them as a group. This might be a senior adult Sunday School class or small group, or even a special event or meal that older members enjoy together. Pastors should show up at these gatherings and use their platform to call

---

3. By "have you thought about" we mean questions like "Have you thought about how you can make a disciple?" or "Have you thought about how you might meet with a younger person in our church to help them follow Jesus?"

people into the work. What are they asking these older people to do? The answer is given in Paul's challenge to Titus.

A primary, though often neglected area where this need is apparent is the pastor's relationship with the older women of the church or the church's women's ministry. A recent rise in resources for women on discipleship has prompted a growing recognition of the need for a discipleship culture in the church. Rightly, young women are hungry for older women to teach them how to follow Jesus and women's ministries are grappling with how to answer this need. Many women's ministry leaders I (Sarah) talk with are diligently working to create a discipleship culture among the women of their church and have shouldered the responsibility to identify and train older women. While this is commendable, there is wisdom in having the direct involvement of the pastors who identify and train the older women of the church. As those responsible for the souls of their congregation (Heb. 13:17), the pastors may have more knowledge of those who have the credibility and capability to disciple younger believers and those who may need more time to be discipled themselves before they begin investing in younger believers.[4] The beauty of a women's ministry is that women's leaders can help connect pastors with the older women of the church so that these saints can be known and called to use their gifts to build up the church.

Pastors may be tempted only to invest themselves in churning out young, competent leaders who will lead churches or go to the nations. While investing in these ways does multiply fruit, they can leave the pastor drained from this challenging work when those capable to disciple the majority of the church are so few. Investing in the older saints of the church is not glamorous. Many of these older saints aren't going to leave to plant a church or be missionaries overseas, but with intentional investment, they can substantially grow the discipling force of the church.

---

4. I (Matt) fear that one of the byproducts of the heinous abuse realities among evangelical leaders is that many pastors approach women with a posture of fear. This fear, combined with the accusations of egalitarian leanings if pastors equip women, leads many to sideline the women of the church rather than invest in them in meaningful ways that honor their value and worth as image bearers and foster their work in discipling other women.

THE PEOPLE AS OLDER SAINTS

It's not just the pastor's job, however. The task of Ephesians 4 is clear—it is the responsibility of the church's pastors to equip the saints for the work of the ministry (Eph. 4:11-16). The imagery of "equipping" is taken from the work of fishermen who would have to mend, or equip their nets for the work.[5] Left to their own, the nets would become tattered and torn so they would be unable to catch fish. Unkempt nets were worthless, so fishermen would have to spend ample time before and after their time on the water to make sure the nets were equipped for the work. The same is true for pastors. Left to their own, church members are not effective in the work of disciple-making, though they might want to be and know they should be. It's the task of the pastor to come alongside his members to equip them for effectiveness. All church members should be equipped for the work of making disciples.

In our church, we've worked to implement the ideas we've suggested in this chapter. I (Sarah) have sought to engage the older women of our church in discipleship for many years, but often heard the push-back of "I don't know enough," or "I'm not

---

5. See a summary of this point in Phil Newton and Rich Shadden, *Mending the Nets* (Greenville: Courier, 2024) 13-14.

equipped to do that," or "I don't know that I'm the right person to disciple someone." A few years ago, we sent a luncheon invitation to specific older women in our church who had observable Christian character and who we knew had been following Jesus for years. Matt started the lunch by highlighting the need for older women to disciple younger women. He encouraged those invited that *they* were the older women of our church and we needed them to take up the call to invest in younger women. At the end of the lunch, we provided ways for them to learn more about what discipleship looks like in practice over the next 8 weeks through training.

After the event, these women admitted that they had previously felt like they weren't needed in the church. After hearing this call from Scripture, their pastor, and other women in the church, they realized that they were a necessary part of God's plan for how the body grows. They were encouraged and felt more equipped when they were reminded of all the tools they possessed—from expositional Sunday sermons, to personal study, to the work of the Spirit, to pastors who want to help, and training offered by others who have practical experience. Older widows were encouraged that part of God's plan for adopting them into this spiritual family is to give them spiritual daughters and granddaughters as they invest in the next generation of Christian women.[6] The call for them to take their place in the family of God at our church and in the narrative of biblical history helped them believe that they were not just relics of by-gone days, but were a vibrant and needed part of our local body.

Our church members testify to the fruit of disciple-making. One older man lamented the fact that he was never discipled in his Christian walk, but a young, college brother approached him for discipleship and he reluctantly agreed. Having no clue where to start, this brother invested in discipleship by simply meeting with this younger man, reading the Word, and talking about their mutual need for obedience and growth. Recognizing a need for discipleship himself, he met with multiple pastors and mature mentors to help with his own needs and questions. Over time, this has become a way of life for this older brother, who now says, "It is my joy to work with other young men in the church

---

6. Psalm 68:6 describes God providing homes for those who are deserted (CSB), or setting the solitary in a home (ESV). This idea provides hope as they live in discipleship relationships for many singles, widows/widowers, and couples unable to have children of their own. Pressing into discipleship unites the church in familial relationships by virtue of their adoption into the family of God.

and show them, by personal experience, how they are called to live according to Scripture." This older man had attended church for many years, heard many sermons, and loved God and His church. It wasn't until meeting with this younger man for a season that his love for God and the church grew as he experienced the love of believers.

An older woman in our church also recounted:

> The call from the pastors and another older woman's specific call for ladies over 40 to join in this training prompted me to step out of my comfort zone. Obviously, at the time, we didn't have many women over 40 in the church, so I did feel the call to be obedient, even though I was apprehensive. After the training, I was matched with a younger woman who had two young toddlers. I didn't have children of my own, so I wondered what I could possibly offer her in a mentoring situation, but I realized I had some wisdom to impart. My mentee's mother was on the mission field. She had a very close relationship with her mother-in-law who lived nearby, but during our time

together, her mother-in-law passed away. Looking back where I had doubts about what I could offer, God didn't have any doubts when He put us together. I have been able to offer encouragement to her and she has been a huge encouragement to me as we've learned from each other and held each other accountable.

The relationship of a discipler and disciple is mutually beneficial. We've seen the following benefits come to those older saints who've heard the call to make disciples and have invested in the work:

- **Love for the Saints**—The time spent investing in each other knits their hearts together with ties of love and care so that the familial nature of the church is lived out in practice.

- **Knowledge of the Word**—As older saints give themselves to the work, their personal devotion shifts from simply consuming the Word to digesting the Word so that they can serve others with the truths they consume.

- **Growth in Confidence**—Older saints press through the insecurity and find that God meets them in the work, which emboldens them to step out in faith in other areas as well.

- **Personal Holiness**—Older saints testify that they get as much as they give. By investing in disciple-making, they have a built-in accountability tool to press them to greater maturity.

- **Investment in the Church**—These church members feel the burden of the work themselves and are far more likely to invest, support, and encourage others (including their pastors) who are laboring to make disciples.

These benefits and testimonies alone will not compel us into the work. We may hear Paul's exhortation and long to embrace this challenge. We want to give our time, energy, and resources to God's mission. We may even long for a prescription that tells us exactly what to do next. Rather than a formula, we get a family. We get people in the church who can walk alongside us and help us to follow Jesus faithfully. Paul gives us a simple path and it's a path that we pray will become well-worn as more and more saints walk along it. We've enjoyed walking this path ourselves.

Over a decade ago, just after having begun a new church in a college community, we invited a young English major to live with us for the summer. She'd been involved in an on-campus ministry we'd led and was attending our church, but we didn't know Jill well at that point. All we knew was that she'd lost her mom to cancer and was thinking about serving as a missionary one day. So, Jill moved into the chaos of our home. She and Sarah made meals and talked about life, and a deep friendship was forged.

After graduating with an English degree, Jill taught for a couple of years before deciding that she would like to take a year to explore international missions. Our church had a developing relationship with a team in Central Asia, so my wife and I traveled over to see if it would be a good fit for Jill. Not long after, she moved, learned language, and began to use her gifts to serve the church. Jill subsequently attended a week-long camp for believers where she met a young, Turkish believer and fell in love. Though we'd been over to visit a number of times, Sarah was soon back on a plane to serve as a bridesmaid in Jill's wedding. Jill and her husband, Ali Can, now have two precious children and have returned to the States where they are active members of our church once again.

The path has not been easy—cross-cultural marriages rarely are. There have been ups and downs, twists and turns, loss, sadness, joy, celebration. And Sarah and I have had front row seats to watch the grace of God change and sanctify Jill. We share this story, not because there's some big, mic-drop moment of transformation. The change agent has been a slow and steady friendship over a long period of time. Of course, there have been Bible studies and conferences and marriage counseling, but the influence of those factors pales in comparison to the significance of human relationships. Intentional relationships over a long period of time between older and younger Christians become a massive catalyst for transformation.

CHAPTER 3

FROM HEART
TO MOUTH

"Older men are to be self-controlled, worthy of respect, sensible, and sound in faith, love, and endurance. In the same way, older women are to be reverent in behavior, not slanderers, not slaves to excessive drinking. They are to teach what is good."
Titus 2:2-3

I (Matt) am a doer. The bigger the project the better. Give me a free Saturday and I'm going to invent something to do. Sometimes it's a task that needs to be done—like home repair projects that seem never to end. Other times, I tear something apart just to make it better. As I'm writing this chapter, I'm frustrated with the state of my garage. It's overrun

with broken bikes, fishing equipment, woodworking tools, camping supplies, and, well, a bunch of
junk. I'm envisioning the glorious Saturday when
the weather warms to pull all of the mess out of that
space, build some shelves, haul a bunch of stuff to
the dump, and make the garage functional again. If
Sarah goes on a trip, she knows that she's going to
come back and something is going to be different
about our house which, I've learned, doesn't always
endear me to my wife.

One of my favorite tasks is yard work. We don't
have a huge yard, so all it takes is a Saturday of work
and I can bring order to the grass, bushes, shrubs,
and plants. I love mowing. If the grass is high, I can
cut a line and immediately look back and note the
progress that I've made. What once looked terrible
now looks great—all in the span of a few seconds.

I'm also a pastor, and if you know anything
about pastoral ministry, you know it works nothing
like cutting grass. The only parallel is the disorder.
People's lives are broken. There's sin and suffering
everywhere. And, if you are a doer like me, your
impulse is to want to fix the mess in a moment. But
it doesn't work that way. In fact, serving people in
the church often looks the exact opposite of mowing grass. You expend a lot of energy to help, and

once you are done, you look back and often aren't sure you made any headway. Or, it seems that something is under control, only for it to grow back even messier overnight.

You don't have to be a doer like me to have read Paul's challenge to older men and older women and want a plan. Paul speaks to older men and older women and we expect the next words to be "Older men you are **to do**..." or "Older women make sure that you **do**..." We seem to naturally want a task list of objectives to fulfill in order to know that we are doing our part to obey the Great Commission.

But notice the next words in Paul's counsel: "Older men are **to be** self-controlled, worthy of respect, sensible, and sound in faith, love and endurance. In the same way, older women are **to be** reverent in behavior, not slanderers, not slaves to excessive drinking" (Titus 2:2-3). The "to be's" come before the "to do's."[1] Before Paul tells them to do anything, he challenges them to be a certain type of person.

---

1. This progression is a natural way to think about all of Christian discipleship. We, first, apply ourselves to becoming a certain type of person and then, out of that "being" we do the things God intends for His people.

CALLED TO BE

Discipleship moves from the heart (who we are) to the mouth (how we teach others). Paul lists fundamental virtues that should be evident in the life of these older Christians. We should not be surprised to read these traits. After all, throughout many cultures there's been a link between the older members of the community and virtue. The older one gets, or so the thought goes, the more wisdom they have acquired along the way. This is why average 13-year-olds are foolish to seek counsel from another teenager. Why go to another equally immature person to seek help? Instead, parents, or even grandparents, have developed the type of character that causes them to be the kind of person you should listen to. In many communal cultures, you still find elders who are sought out for their insight due to the perception that they are men or women of virtue.

Paul provides a list of the traits you should find in older men and women in the church. It does not seem that these lists are meant to be all-inclusive. We don't think that Paul intends to list every virtue that older saints should possess, but these are a sampling of the life-patterns that set older men and women off as exemplary. In other words, the character of older men and older women should cause younger men and women to want to be like them when they grow up.

These characteristics are not just for older men and women. These traits are evidence of the Spirit's activity in these individuals' lives. In fact, you could rightly see these traits as synonyms for the more common fruit of the Spirit list found in Galatians 5:22-23). It makes sense that this list is true for all Christians, since you must start walking the path toward these virtues at a younger age if you hope to arrive at them when you are older.

There is also a strong parallel to the qualifications of a pastor—where character and virtue are foremost concerns (1 Tim. 3:1-7; Titus 1:5-9). Pastors are to be exemplary older men who set an example for the other older men in the church.

Paul's list isn't happenstance. Note the traits he mentions for older men—self-control, respectability, sensibility, soundness in faith, love, and endurance. There's a direct link between the first trait and verse 6 where Paul exhorts older men to instill self-control in younger men. In short, Paul challenges older men to be the kind of man they want to teach other men to become. It's critical that older men model in their lives what they want to pass on to others. Or spun another way, it's virtually impossible to train someone else to be something you, yourself, are not also becoming.

Sarah and I both enjoy going to the gym. For the last five years, we work out together multiple times a week and do so at a gym with coaches that we love and trust. Not only are the coaches strong, but many times they get in the mix and do the daily workout with us. Honestly, it would be difficult to take guidance and correction from someone who was not also working hard to pursue physical discipline.

There are carry-over examples in all aspects of life. An older man may have great skill with investments and savings as he approaches retirement. He might be able to teach another younger man to model his retirement portfolio. He could likely set the man up with an investment strategy that rivals his own. But what happens if this same older man is discontent and covetous? The older man may be able to teach good patterns, but he will be hard-pressed to influence the heart.

Or what about the older woman who developed a business that allowed her to provide financially while raising a family. This woman might be able to meet with other young women to help them hone their entrepreneurial skills. But what if that same woman is plagued by anxiety and fear? What if she copes with the pressure with a hidden addiction? Again, this woman may be able to help another young woman master certain behaviors, but we all know that you reproduce who you are and not just what you do, so it will be difficult for this older woman to make any lasting difference in another person's life.

The same is true for disciple-making. You can teach people to read the Bible or share their faith, but without a corresponding pattern of life, your words will fall flat. Even worse, those listening to you talk will see the disconnect between what you say and what you do and will likely be repelled by the hypocrisy they observe.

NOT A CALL TO BE PERFECT

Here's a place to address a concern that will derail many readers from applying the counsel of this book. People intuitively know that our character is more important than our actions; and many people know there are dark places of hypocrisy hidden under the polished exterior of our lives. We know that if we invite people into our lives and invest in them then they will see the real us. And, rather than bringing our sin into the light, repenting of our hypocrisy, and seeking to change, we simply shut other people out so we can coddle our sin rather than apply the gospel to our shame.

But think about what happens if we reverse the logic here. Rather than thinking that we can't let other people get close because of our sin, what if a primary means God provides for addressing our sin is other people? Maybe God wants to use the presence of other people to cause us to feel the weight of our sin so that we turn from it. This point is commonly made regarding marriage. God uses marriage—the presence of another human in close proximity—to help you see your sin and bring about your sanctification. The idea does not merely hold for married couples. A spouse can aid our sanctification, but so also does the presence of younger men and younger women in our lives. When we invite other people to really know us, their presence provides steady pressure to attend to our own hearts.

Older men and women don't gain this respectable character overnight, but through years of recognizing sin, confessing it, and repenting of it, they put off the old man and put on the new (Col. 3:9-10). We are qualified to pass on sound doctrine not on the basis of perfection but because we give ourselves to the daily work of relying on the Holy

Spirit to guide, strengthen, and comfort us with the promises of God.

MARKS OF MATURITY IN AN OLDER MAN

Self-control is first on the list. The term here refers to having power over yourself. In contrast to someone who requires an authority figure standing over him to do what is right, a man marked by self-control knows how to bring himself under God's authority. The Word of God and the Spirit of God are enough to bring control to the man's sinful appetites. Self-control, or the lack thereof, is unique evidence of the Spirit's work in the life of a man. Like untamed horses, unregenerate or immature men tend to be enslaved by their passions.[2]

It's easy to see why self-control would be linked with age. In infancy, children have virtually no self-control. They are all impulse and instinct. Whatever urge they feel is acted on, often with no restraint. Children follow the same pattern. We have five children, and for us it wasn't the terrible 2s, but the terrible 4s through 8s. Those years were defined

---

2. For a wonderful treatment on the subject of self-control and masculinity see J. C. Ryle, *Thoughts for Young Men* (Edinburgh: Banner of Truth, 2015).

by the steady battle to bring our children under authority. They often did what they wanted when they wanted to, with little concern for the impact their actions would have on others or the consequences their actions might have for their lives. Self-control doesn't naturally grow as the child nears puberty, either. If you've been around a prepubescent boy you know that even their bodies just flop around. They are often awkward and clumsy as they morph into adults. So it's no wonder that Paul mentions self-control as the primary trait that an older man is to instill in younger men (v. 6). It's the area that most young men lack and, presumably, it's the area that older men have had the most time to cultivate.

Next, Paul says that older men "*must be worthy of respect*" (v. 2). The language here is important. Older men are often respected by virtue of their age. Let a refined older man walk into a room, and there's often a natural deference to him. The key word here is "*worthy.*" He does not say that a man should simply be respected by virtue of his age, but that he should be worthy of respect. In other words, his character should make it right and proper for people to look up to him. In many cultures, it's expected that people stand up to show honor to a respectable older man when he enters the room.

We don't have to survey the cultural landscape for long to note how important and, sadly, rare such a mark is for older men. It's increasingly common to hear horror stories of older men who lived with secret sin for decades only to be outed later in life. Many of these men were prominent leaders in the broader culture and even in the church.[3]

While self-control focuses on the man's relationship with himself, respectability highlights the perspective of outsiders on the man's life. Paul makes a similar point when writing to Timothy regarding the qualifications of elders. There he says elders "must have a good reputation among outsiders, so that he does not fall into disgrace and the devil's trap" (1 Tim. 3:7). And Peter makes the same point regarding all Christians: "Dear friends, I urge you as strangers and exiles to abstain from sinful desires that wage war against the soul. Conduct yourselves honorably among the Gentiles, so that when they slander you as evildoers, they will observe your good works and will glorify God on the day he visits" (1 Pet 2:11-12). Christians live in the public arena where unbelievers can, and should, observe their lives. Writing about ancient Israel, Michael Goheen

---

3. See Michael J. Kruger, *Bully Pulpit: Confronting the Problem of Spiritual Abuse in the Church* (Grand Rapids: Zondervan, 2022).

suggests that the nation was called to be a shop window where people could observe the glory of God and the transformation He brings to people.[4] This principle is also true within the church. Older men should live as a shop window where younger men can observe a life of virtue.

The third trait on the list is sensibility. This word is a close synonym to self-control, which in and of itself emphasizes how important self-control is. Sensibility speaks of being under control, measured, stable, or ordered. This type of man is not driven to and fro by his passions and lusts. He's not impulsive in the decisions he makes in life. He's a man who does what is right because it is right; and because he acts rightly, he can lead young men to do the same.

The final qualification of the traits of an older man is a three-fold list of faith, love, and endurance. None of these virtues should be a surprise. There's a close connection here to the way Paul concludes his famous chapter in 1 Corinthians: "Now these three remain: faith, hope, and love—but the greatest of these is love" (v. 13). Paul wants older men who

---

4. See Michael Goheen and Craig Bartholomew, *The Drama of Scripture: Finding Our Place in the Biblical Story* (Baker: Grand Rapids: 2004).

have a deep faith in God, a love for God and their fellow man (Matt. 22:37-40), and hopeful endurance to run the race to the end (Heb. 12:1-2).

As he did earlier with the idea of respect, Paul here modifies these three virtues by saying that older men should be "sound" in faith, love, and endurance. Sound means healthy or whole. An older man is sure to have to attend to his physical health. More doctors visits, blood tests, and procedures mark the aging process. Ideally, the older man goes to meet with the doctor who reports that the man is healthy—all of the markers came back within range. Cholesterol is good. Sugar is fine. Nothing abnormal to report. Praise God! Well, Paul here imagines a doctor checking on an older man and looking for faith, love, and endurance and finding that the man is sound. He's healthy and whole.

MARKS OF MATURITY IN AN OLDER WOMAN

Paul then does the same for the ladies. He says they, too, are called to embody certain virtues. There's an unmissable implication here that demands highlighting in our current, cultural moment. Gender exists and gender matters. Such a point would hardly need to have been made a few decades ago, but the normative assumption today is that gender is non-existent, irrelevant, and changeable.

The Bible does not allow such a dismissive attitude toward gender. In fact, gender is God's design. He is the one who made them male and female and declared these gender categories were good (Gen. 1:26-31). Gender isn't a result of sin and the fall, but an essential way that God designed His image bearers. Here, in Paul's writing, it's a fundamental way that God uses these image bearers to make disciples in the church. It's clear that Paul is intentional to select traits that are vital for older men and other traits that are essential for older women. We should not interpret this to mean that Paul thinks that women don't need to be self-controlled or that men should not avoid slander. Nor does he mean to imply that older men can't have a positive spiritual impact on younger women or older women on younger men. Instead, it seems he's shining a spotlight on certain facets of life that older men and older women need to give particular attention to and thereby transmit to those of the same gender.

First, older women are to be reverent in behavior. They are to act appropriately, in ways that show themselves to be set apart to God. This doesn't mean a woman must have a bland personality or be demure in public. But it does mean that she carries herself with respect and honor.

We've all likely had the experience of seeing someone in a context that we had not seen them before—like the first time you bump into your teacher in the supermarket or when you see your doctor at a ballgame. It's fine for a teacher or doctor to be out in public, but it's still weird at first. But what's not acceptable is for the teacher or the doctor to act inappropriately in these spaces. The teacher can't steal food at the market and the doctor shouldn't yell curses at the referee. Such behavior is not appropriate for the role. Paul makes this point regarding older Christian women. They should carry themselves with dignity and honor. Elsewhere Paul counsels all Christians to "walk worthy of the calling you have received" (Eph. 4:1). Older women set the example in this regard. They walk worthy of their calling as Christians and their position in culture.

He then continues by pointing out the danger of slander (v. 3). In the same way that self-control in areas of lust or anger can be a unique temptation for men, so can women be uniquely predisposed to sin with their tongue. James warns about the unique challenge of such sin (Jam. 3:1-12). Words can act to spark a great fire or they can work as fertilizer, bringing life to many. Older women are called to use their words to build up and promote health. It is not enough that they avoid using their words to gossip or slander. In contrast to the rebellious Cretans, who are described in Titus 1 as "full of empty talk and deception," older women are positioned to speak life in the culture.

Paul also calls older women to refrain from excessive drinking. This was likely a unique temptation for older women since they had more discretionary time and declining health. Excessive drinking was also rampant among younger women in Cretan culture, so older women were called to moderation in an effort to set an example for these ladies. Perhaps more important to note is the language of enslavement. Throughout the Bible, sin is pictured as slavery (Jn. 8:34). To sin is to be a slave to sin, so these older women are free from such slavery to alcohol and presumably from other areas as well. This allows them to set an example for the younger women of how to escape such enslavement.

Older men and women are to focus on becoming a certain type of person. They are, first, to be someone. Then they are to do something.

CALLED TO TEACH

I (Matt) can get away with writing this story because my wife freely tells it. She was three years younger and still in college when we got married. She'd never lived on her own, and cooking was never a priority or need. She just went to the cafeteria and grabbed something to eat. But now we were married and it was on us to make our own food. So Sarah sought help. She asked two older ladies to train her to cook. She wasn't striving to be a chef; she merely wanted to learn how to make a few basic meals. They picked two meals, and she asked these ladies to show her the process all the way from grocery shopping until the finished meal made it to the table. These women mentored my wife in the art of cooking.

Now you might imagine another way this could have played out. We could have simply invited ourselves to have a meal with these ladies who were skillful cooks. We'd enjoy the fruits of the labor, but not learn to cook. Not bad, but not great for our home long term either. More than a meal, Sarah wanted help learning how to cook.

That's how Paul ends this part of his call to older men and women. They are not merely to be exemplary Christians, but they "are to teach what is good" (Titus 2:3). Now that he's told them what they are to be, older saints are then given an assign-ment. In context, "good" refers to the pattern of virtue that exudes from their lives and spills over into applied wisdom and godly living. And it's this spill-over effect that God uses to help younger men and women grow. Christians strive to become a cer-tain type of person and invite others to join them in that pursuit (1 Cor. 11:1). As they earn the right to instruct others through living a transformed life, disciple-makers are then poised to obey the next as-pect of Paul's instructions to Titus.

CHAPTER 4

FROM EXAMPLE TO TRAINING

"...so that they may encourage the young women to love their husbands and to love their children, to be self-controlled, pure, workers at home, kind, and in submission to their husbands, so that God's word will not be slandered. In the same way, encourage the young men to be self-controlled in everything."
Titus 2:4-6

My (Sarah) mom passed away in a tragic accident when I was 19 years old. Four months later, I began dating my now husband, Matt. Two years later, we were married. As a 19-year-old, I had not planned to lose my mom, nor had I planned to be married so soon after her death and I realized the great loss of not asking more questions or paying more attention to the ways she lived out these Titus 2 characteristics. During our engagement, I recognized the need to seek practical advice about keeping house and marriage, but without my mom around to ask, I turned to key older, believing women in my family and church for help. As Matt mentioned previously, two women taught me to make a nice meal, from grocery store to table, since I didn't know the different cuts of meat or how to find my way around the grocery store. I asked questions and learned helpful tips from observing my step-mother as she straightened, organized, and cleaned her home. Sprinkled throughout these instructions I learned how to use my home for hospitality as a steward of this gift that God had given. My aunt taught me that a loving marriage is built by daily choices to serve, support, and build up your spouse. These older women gathered around me on my wedding day where my mom would have been—prepping my hair and makeup, placing the "something borrowed" and "something blue." They mothered me during some of the most important moments of my life.

The same knowledge could have been gained through attending a class or Googling for answers, but life-on-life training provided space for practice, failure, correction, and greater honing of skill as I grew more proficient. This ongoing process is necessary for any genuine teaching to take place.

God's Word is sufficient for life and godliness (2 Pet. 1:3), and He kindly gives us models to follow so we can see His wisdom in the flesh as it is lived out in obedient, faithful lives. But training in godliness is not just caught, it is taught as well. Paul instructs older women to engage younger women with this type of teaching that corresponds to godly living.

Such godly living was vital in a place like Crete. Paul described the Cretans as "liars, evil beasts, and lazy gluttons" (Titus 1:12). This cultural reality meant that those who came to faith in Jesus Christ had a long road of sanctification ahead of them. New Cretan believers needed to be trained in how to put off lying and embrace purity in their speech, reject their habits of evil and pursue kindness, mercy, and love, and deny their former impulses and instead to put on self-control. These new believers left the cultural trappings they grew up in and the families who taught them, to pursue a new family in Christ and needed spiritual parents who would pass down sound doctrine and godly living. Teaching what is good would create a distinctly Christian culture in contrast to the surrounding pagan culture. Though our historical context has changed significantly, the same underlying patterns are at play. People leave their former way of life (Eph. 4:22) and pursue Christ-likeness, and the best way to see growth is with an older man or woman walking alongside them to help.

A WORD ON TRAINING

Before we look at the themes Paul lists in this section, first a word about training. We've already mentioned that in verse 3 Paul says older men and women are to "teach." In most of our contexts, that word comes pre-loaded with mental assumptions on our part. When we think of teaching, we think of something that happens in a classroom when a formal expert (the teacher) stands before a room of students and gives a prepared lecture. When applied to disciple-making, this classroom model of teaching makes many Christians feel insecure about their ability to actually make disciples since they don't see themselves as experts, nor would they want to stand in front of a room and lecture.

While there is a collection of truth from God's Word to be communicated, the method of teaching Paul argues for in Titus 2 seems to be something different altogether. In verses 4 and 7 he uses the word "encourage" to speak of the task he's giving to older men and women. Literally, he wants them to walk alongside younger men and women and impart courage to them. The virtues themselves speak of this life-on-life pattern as well since traits like self-control or kindness are not those that can be embodied by merely listening to a lecture on the subject. The picture is of a trusted guide walking alongside a novice along a tricky hike. The guide, knowing the challenges of the hike and the scenic opportunities "teaches" along the way by communicating vital truth at just the right moment. The older man or older woman in Titus 2 is such a spiritual guide.

Imagine if all you had were a podium and a 50-minute time block to deliver a lecture to 30 students on how to become self-controlled, the trait Paul commends older men to pass on to younger men in this passage. You could certainly give a quality lecture on the subject the way you might describe an international destination you visited on a recent trip. You could tell the students all about the ancient Greek notion of virtue and how Aristotle or Plato described the excellent life. You could even survey biblical texts that speak of discipline or the fruit of the Spirit and help your students understand how grace empowers sanctification. None of this would be a waste of time and some high capacity students might be able to take the lectures and appropriate the truth they heard to their lives in meaningful ways. But is this the sole or best option? We don't think so.

Our family started doing CrossFit about 6 years ago. No need to fear, we aren't in a cult. But we really enjoyed the discipline, the challenge, and the benefits we saw to our health and energy when we were in the gym regularly. As many will tell you, though, that's not the best part about a workout setting like CrossFit. It's the people. You make friends. You find community. There's something about almost dying doing burpees and wall balls that bonds you with people. In particular, we love the coaches.

If I'm honest, up to the time I entered the gym, I probably couldn't have told you what a muscle-up or high hang power clean was, much less how to do one. My coaches did not simply design a computer presentation that outlined the mechanics of these exercises. They did not gather a group of moderately overweight and massively out of shape clients for a semester long course. They did two things. First, they modeled the lift themselves—slowing down to describe the various posture and muscle groups engaged along the way. Then they watched me do the lift and corrected the numerous flaws in my movements. I then did the lift again, each time receiving correction and redirection until, after years of practice, I'm moderately decent at the exercises and could likely teach others to do them well.

What if we thought about discipleship the same way? What if the goal was not merely to produce older men and women who were skilled lecturers and teachers but coaches and trainers? This paradigm seems to be what Paul models in 2 Timothy: "But you have followed my teaching, conduct, purpose, faith, patience, love, and endurance, along with the persecutions and sufferings" (3:10-11). He steadily exhorts people to "imitate me, as I also imitate Christ' (1 Cor. 11:1). Paul was a discipleship coach of sorts and he wanted the men and women to whom he was writing to do the same. First, he encourages older women to train younger women to do a few things.

WOMEN, LOOK TO THE HOME

The implication of teaching "what is good" will first work itself out in the woman's closest relationships—those found in her home. Older women are to teach younger women to love their husbands and children.

We have to grapple with a common objection here. Is Paul merely reflecting on a patriarchal culture in which men worked and women stayed back to care for the home and raise children? Are older women merely to help others live domesticated lives? In order to answer these questions we must say two equally true things that are not mutually exclusive though they may seem to be on the surface.[1]

On the one hand, Paul is certainly writing in a specific cultural context that is different from our own. So his exhortation here should not be interpreted as implying that these are the only areas that women need to consider or the only context in which their sanctification will be seen. He's merely challenging older women to apply the gospel to younger women in the way they would most commonly spend their time, and thereby work out their salvation in that context. This list is not meant to be exhaustive, but Paul instructs Titus that older women should apply the gospel to the unique contexts of

---

1. We acknowledge that our society does not currently excel at saying two true things at once. We're drawn to creating stark "either-or" divisions with mutually exclusive choices even though most of adult life necessitates the ability to think both-and and not either-or.

marriage and parenting.[2] This will look like teaching single women how to apply the gospel to their context of singleness, encouraging them to love the next generation in their local church body. It could also take the form of an older widow teaching a younger woman whose husband has left how the gospel applies in the context she finds herself. Thus, we should be able to appropriately extrapolate these ideals to other areas, such as working outside of the home or attending to relationships with others beyond her immediate family.

On the other hand, Paul's voice to women in this passage does provide clarity and credence to a vital component of God's design for womanhood. In an age where it's seemingly disparaging to speak of femininity in these domesticated terms, there is

---

2. Does this mean that single women cannot disciple? We don't think so. Since Paul commends discipleship in the normative context of women in the culture, we do not believe he is suggesting that this is the only place or people who can disciple. Single women have much to commend as older saints. They can certainly invest in younger women, even younger women who are married or who have kids. While there may be limitations on what they can teach or train from personal example, the fruit of the Spirit and godly wisdom isn't limited to those who are married or who have kids. In many cases, however, it may be wise for older, single women (and men) to seek out younger, single women or men for discipleship. This shared station in life likely provides for a shared context that makes application more natural.

value in commending the dignity and worth in-herent in the work of loving a spouse and raising children. Many women will give substantial time to supporting a husband and raising kids; this is hon-orable work—and a primary context where sancti-fication is seen.

Here again, the value of life-on-life training over classroom teaching is clearly seen. The word used here for "love" signifies an affectionate fond-ness for the object of that love. Wives and mothers can relate to the common temptation to love their family by serving them, managing the home, com-pleting the necessary tasks, but devoid of a fond af-fection for the husband or children they are serving. After the 4th or 5th time of crawling out of bed in the middle of the night to feed a squalling newborn, affections can wane. Older women in the church can testify to the fact that this season doesn't last forever and can lend courage to the younger woman to endure faithfully, seeing their newborn as a gift from God and this season as a gift from God for her sanctification.

Similarly, after a disagreement with her hus-band, an older woman can ask the wife to remem-ber what she loves about her husband, to give thanks to the Lord for him, and to pursue reconciliation through repentance and forgiveness. The older woman can recall times of disagreement in her own marriage and how the Lord used the pursuit of reconciliation to draw her closer to her husband. These are difficult ideas to teach from the front of a classroom as an expert and require vulnerability, honesty, and reliance on the Lord and His word to convey.

Paul also instructs older women to encourage the young women to submit to their husbands. There is much wisdom in women teaching other women how to submit to their own husbands. Our pastors are currently preaching through 1 Peter, and during a recent Sunday morning gathering, Matt preached to the gathered body on 1 Peter 3:1-6: "Wives, submit yourselves to your own husbands...". This sermon was then strengthened as women taught other women about how they were obeying Peter's counsel in their marriages. This woman-to-woman instruction provided an added level of credibility and experience to the expository sermon that was preached. When a woman extols the benefit and beauty of submission, the younger woman tends to hear with receptive ears.

Lastly, older women are to teach younger women to be workers at home. In our context, there are many young women with so much discretionary time that they spend on social media deep dives, binging on streaming platforms, or a plethora of other escapes. Other women may experience seasons of working outside of the home, which drastically reduces the energy they're able to give in the home. Like the Proverbs 31 woman who manages her home and entrepreneurial work, women in all circumstances will need instruction on how to manage their time, how to manage and complete household tasks so that their needs and the needs of the household are met, and how to steward the gift of their home for God's glory in areas like hospitality.

In a culture where the home is fractured and where the absence of the nuclear family is a foregone conclusion for most, Christian women who look to their home and the relationships in it will stand out. When Christian women tend to the relationships in their home in a Christlike way, those relationships will flourish and will demonstrate ordered, harmonious relationships as they were intended to be. As these women manage their homes and open them for hospitality in the church, they display the generosity of God to a watching world.

WOMEN, LOOK
TO YOUR CHARACTER

Paul doesn't only emphasize the younger woman in her home but also addresses her character, instructing older women to encourage the young women to be self-controlled, pure, and kind. Again, older women with similar pressures, experiences, and seasons of life speak into the lives of younger women providing great wisdom and credibility.

An easy temptation for everyone is to think that your sin flows out of your unique pressures. Maybe you've heard from another woman, "Well, if my husband would just put his dirty clothes in the hamper instead of right next to the hamper, I wouldn't get so angry!" Or, "If God would just give me a husband, I would have someone to fill my time and wouldn't waste it so much." Or, "I lashed out because my hormones are out of whack and it's hard to control what comes out of my mouth." Scripture teaches that no temptation has overtaken us that is not common to man (1 Cor. 10:13), and the temptation to excuse our sin based on our unique pressures is common. While older women can identify with those unique pressures, they can come alongside the younger woman to help her see that the fight for holiness in spite of those pressures is right, good, and worth the effort.

Proverbs 25:28 says, "A man without self-control is like a city broken into and left without walls." Self-control is a protection for us keeping us from influences that seek to harm us and keeping us from running straight into sin. A lack of self-control leads to destruction for us and others in our lives. For their sake and ours, we must learn and teach others how to practice self-control by the power of the Spirit. From a young age, we begin to teach our children this virtue by instructing, "You may not hit your sister. Use self-control to keep your hands to yourself." As we mature, we still need teaching on self-control but it sounds more like, "It is unwise for you to skip your daily time in God's Word for more sleep. Use self-control so that you go to bed earlier and are able to wake up with enough time to meet with the Lord." The accountability and wisdom from older believers helps to change our perspective so that we live self-controlled lives.

In Psalm 24:3-4, David asks, "Who can ascend the hill of the Lord?" and answers with, "He who has clean hands and a pure heart." Many things tempt women to be divided in their thinking and actions. Christian influencers on social media who speak unbiblical things about God tempt women to impure doctrine. The cares of this world—how to keep our skin smooth and youthful, the right foods to eat and workout regimens to stay healthy and strong, even the best ways to care for your sourdough starter—can cloud our undivided love for God. Single women and married women need help loosening their grip on believing that romantic love will fill their longings and instead devote themselves to Jesus, who alone will satisfy. We need older women to train younger women and to model for them pure devotion to God in mind, body, and emotions.

Maybe you've heard the phrase, "If mama ain't happy, ain't nobody happy." If you happen to be in a household where "mama ain't happy," kindness is probably the furthest character trait from reality at that moment. Why is this characteristic highlighted in Titus out of all that could be chosen from the list of the fruit of the Spirit? Kindness is a heart to mouth path where what is rehearsed in the heart will come out of the mouth. If the heart is full of selfishness, bitterness, resentment, envy, or gossip, kind words will not flow. Instead, words of complaint, anger, frustration, irritability, and unkindness will spew. But if the heart is full of thankfulness, humility, service, and looking to the interests of others, kind words will be readily available. Describing a noble wife in Proverbs 31:26, Solomon says, "She opens her mouth with wisdom, and the teaching of kindness is on her tongue." As a woman's words exude kindness to her husband, her children, and the many relationships God gives her, she reflects His great kindness (Romans 2:4). The Holy Spirit can convict our hearts as we listen to that woman thoughtfully and intentionally speak with kindness to her sisters at church, her neighbors, her husband, or her children. The more we're around her, the more we see God's kindness reflected in her and the more her pattern of speech influences and encourages kindness in our own speech.

As I (Sarah) have entered my 40s, I've heard more and more stories of the ills of menopause. Some stories about flashes of heat and anger can be comical, others involving the lack of filter and uncomfortable bodily changes sound miserable, and all have induced some anxiety in Matt as he wonders how I might face the next season of life looming in front of me. Aging well is a discipleship issue. A few women in my church have pointed out that my story is informed by the gospel and the Spirit's work in my life, not by the changes to come. They have challenged the notion that aging necessitates the loss of a filter by teaching that as I walk with the Spirit, I will not gratify the desires of my sinful nature. My fears of what might come have been comforted as they remind me of Jesus who loves me, invites me to come to Him for rest when I'm weary and heavy-laden and has promised to never leave me or forsake me. These women remind me that my season or circumstances of life don't define me, but what God says about me does. They encourage me with the hope of sanctification and spur me on to persevere as we wait together for future glorification.

MEN, LOOK TO YOUR SELF-CONTROL

The structure of this passage places character and conduct instruction from older women to younger women (v. 3-5) in between the role of older men in verse 2 and the instruction to younger men in verse 6. What's striking about the direction here is the simplicity. Paul tells older men to do one thing—to help younger men exercise self-control. That's it!

Perhaps the simplicity here is rooted in the fact that young men can't do more than one thing at once. More likely, however, is the reality that self-control is a root issue for young men that impacts every other aspect of their lives. This point would seem substantiated by the tag "in everything" that starts verse 7. If you teach young men to be self-controlled in everything then you are essentially teaching them to work out their sanctification in every area of life.

It's no wonder to see self-control here. Paul also includes it in his famous list of the fruit of the Spirit (Gal. 5:22-23). It is, after all, the final fruit in the list. Paul uses self-control to describe the sum total of a life well lived:

> Don't you know that the runners in a stadium all race, but only one receives the prize? Run in such a way to win the prize. Now everyone who competes exercises self-control in everything. They do it to receive a perishable crown, but we an imperishable crown. So I do not run like one who runs aimlessly or box like one beating the air. Instead, I discipline my body and bring it under strict control, so that after preaching to others, I myself will not be disqualified (1 Cor. 9:24-27).

The essential means of glorifying God in all things is self-control. Through self-control, men renounce the evil passions that war against godliness and train themselves to pursue God and godliness. In fact, this is exactly how Paul concludes this section of his letter to Titus:

> For the grace of God has appeared, bringing salvation for all people, instructing us to deny godlessness and worldly lusts and to live in a sensible, righteous, and godly way in the present age, while we wait for the blessed hope, the appearing of the glory of our great God and Savior, Jesus Christ. He gave himself for us to redeem us from all lawlessness and to cleanse for himself a people for his own possession, eager to do good works (Titus 2:11-14).

Self-control directs our affections to God.

There's no surprise that this virtue is necessary for young men. If you've ever met a high school boy, you know that self-control isn't the first trait that comes to mind. In fact, you might suggest that young males "lack self-control in everything." They are often hedonists to the max. They do what they want when they want to do it, a habit that often leads to an unchecked desire for pleasure. For example, if you take a typical 14-year-old boy and leave him at home alone for a full day, it's unlikely that you'll come home to find he's cleaned up the house, washed the dishes, and worked diligently on his schoolwork. Instead, he may have squandered the day in triviality.

The older man's task is simple and it's complex. How do you coach a young man toward virtue?

We will say more on this in future chapters, but some comments are in order here. First, in order for older men to train younger men in self-control, these older men must be self-controlled themselves. This point bears repeating. Older men have to be a certain type of person before they can teach others to do the same. This does not mean that the older man perfectly demonstrates self-control. Such a standard would be impossible to uphold. But it does mean that the general tenor of the man's life should be self-control. It also means that the older man should quickly and willingly repent when he fails to model this virtue.

Fathers have an essential role to play here. Because of their God-ordained role in the lives of their sons and the sheer volume of time that sons will spend with their father, discipling a young man to embrace self-control is an essential component of the father's task as an older man. Many times a father's lack of self-control has generational implications for his children (Ex. 34:6-7). At minimum, if the father is not self-controlled enough to invest in his son, then that lack of parental intentionality will likely have long range implications. One could argue that one of the primary reasons more older men are not more engaged in discipling younger men is because they were never discipled by their fathers.

Since the work of disciple-making has often not happened in the home, the local church needs more and more men to step up as surrogate grandfathers and fathers to the men in the church.

Finally, in order to teach someone to be self-controlled, that person must have access to your life. An older man cannot merely commend self-control from a distance, he must model a life of discipline for the younger man. This act of modeling seems to be a critical missing ingredient in the work of disciple-making, particularly in an American church context.

So it goes, older men and women of character invest their lives into training other, younger men and women to follow their example. These older saints will not be able to do this work alone. Thankfully Jesus' himself promised the Holy Spirit to be the power source that fuels this mission (Acts 1:8). Equipped with that power, believers can be confident that training younger saints is not only necessary, but possible.

CHAPTER 5

FROM ONCE IN A WHILE TO ALL OF THE TIME

"Make yourself an example of good works with integrity and dignity in your teaching."
Titus 2:7

The joy of parenting is unrivaled—God gives us little human lives, filled with potential. And you, as the parent, get the privilege of working to shape that little life into a fully formed adult who is capable of functioning well in the world. The privilege is matched by the weight of the responsibility. There's so much to do. So much you want your child to embrace. So far to go. So where do you start? How do you take one small, little step forward? What do you do first? All parents know that there is not a linear answer to this question. You simply cannot approach parenting like a math equation: Do A, then do B, followed by C, and you'll raise a healthy, well-adjusted child. Parenting doesn't work that way.

Neither does disciple-making. We're tempted to look for a clearly defined process that is guaranteed to make disciples. This motive lies behind the constant hunt for another book or resource or curriculum plan to guide the disciple-making process. We're not suggesting that such tools aren't helpful.[1] The distinction between helpful and unhelpful resources seems related to whether or not the tool fosters the type of life-on-life mentorship Paul describes in Titus 2.

I (Matt) was a chubby kid, and chubby kids in my hometown played football. To be specific, the chubby kids played on the offensive line. My role was simple—push people out of the way so the actual athletes could take the ball and make the play. All that changed one week. We had a terrible game the Friday before. Our tackling was awful. So

---

[1.] This suggestion would undermine the fact that I (Matt) have worked to write quality books that teach methods to aid in discipleship. My two workbooks entitled *Aspire* and my basic Bible reading plan, *The Seven Arrows*, are tools that I've seen God use mightily over the years.

the coach lined us up in two opposing lines about twenty yards apart. The first man in the line, regardless of his position, picked up the ball and ran and the first person in the opposite line tackled him. We did this for two hours. Time after time, chunky boys like me who never touched the ball had to do our best to survive the ferocious hit of an oncoming linebacker running at full speed. I never wanted to touch the ball again.

There's a similar temptation in the work of disciple-making. There are those who are presumed to be skilled disciple-makers—pastors, ministry leaders, small group leaders, and Sunday school teachers. Within the church, we assume these key leaders are going to make the play by discipling the masses. So we give them the ball all of the time. They stand on stages and preach sermons. They lead groups through inductive Bible studies. They meet with people in private for counsel and care. What happens over time, however, is that the rest of the church learns to be passive. Their role in disciple-making, if they even think of it as such, is simply to make it possible for the skilled disciplers to do the work. This passivity sidelines many of the older men and women in the church. Then, if they do get a chance to invest in disciple-making, we discover we have under-prepared and poorly equipped them for the work, so when it goes badly, they think that they never want to try that again.

When we look at books and resources, we want to leverage these tools to adequately equip all of those in the church to feel competent to do the work. Even good sermons should have a mobilizing effect among the church. I often tell our church that my aim is that they'd listen to my sermons with their ears and their mouth. Ears to hear what God has to say for them. A mouth to consider how they can take the Word that's preached and share it with others. To do this, older men and women will need to see disciple-making as a way of life—something they do all of the time and not just once in a while.

LIFE AND DOCTRINE

Notice where Paul goes next in verse 7. He's just told Titus to find older men and women who exemplify godliness. These older men are to cultivate self-control in younger men and older women are to instill virtue in younger women. How?

Once again Paul presses personal ownership. "Make yourself an example…". We've seen this pattern throughout Titus 2. He focused on the maturity of the older men and older women throughout.

He tells them to be the type of person they want the younger man or woman to become.

This is parenting 101. We *can* tell our kids to become something we are not. We have a term for that—hypocrite. People follow your example long before they submit to your instruction. In fact, if your teaching and example are not in line, your example will often undermine your teaching. Notice the direction Paul provides. He tells these older men and women to "make" themselves an example. This is a term of intentionality. It's not merely being an example but intentionally setting oneself up as an example. It may seem that making yourself an example is a statement of pride. "Hey, look at me. Watch how mature I am." This type of showboating is surely prideful, but we need not make ourselves an example in this way. We can simply, humbly follow Jesus and invite others into the good work God's grace is producing in our lives.

This seems to be the very thing Paul did throughout his ministry. Consider the way he reflects on his work among the Thessalonians:

> Although we could have been a burden as
> Christ's apostles, instead we were gentle
> among you, as a nurse nurtures her own

children. We cared so much for you that
we were pleased to share with you not
only the gospel of God but also our own
lives, because you had become dear to us
(1 Thess. 2:7-8).

Paul was only able to minister among the Christians
in Thessalonica for a few months before he was run
out of the city by a violent mob (Acts 17:1-9). Even
though the time was short, Paul says the people became very dear to him, such that he treated them as
a mother treats her newborn. His care was evident
in two ways: 1) He shared the gospel with them,
and 2) He shared his own life. This dual focus lies
at the heart of Paul's exhortation for older men and
women to make themselves examples and to do so
through their good works and their good teaching
(Titus 2:7).

We might be helped to think of good works
and good teaching as the two wings on a plane, both
of which are essential if you hope to avoid crashing.
Those who fly in disciple-making will utilize faithful teaching and godly lives to create a lifestyle fer-
mented with disciple-making intentionality.

WING #1: FAITHFUL TEACHING

In our day, good teaching is easy to access. While not every local church has faithful preaching or teaching, the ease of digital technology allows us to find someone who is faithful with the gospel, has a unique approach or perspective, and is an effective communicator. With the press of a button, that teaching can fill our AirPods everywhere we go. Even within our churches, it's common for older men or women to teach in a group setting. Whether from pulpits, classroom podiums, or home Bible studies and small groups, the normative approach is one on many and the teaching model is a one-way lecture. Healthy teaching and preaching is a gift of God's grace, and we should praise the Lord that we live at a time where we can feast on God's Word through faithful pastors and teachers. This is especially true when that preaching comes from faithful pastors in the local church of which you are a member. There, the weekly pulpit is providing a steady diet of gospel truth that nourishes and enriches the soul.

The wing of faithful teaching is necessary, but not sufficient, for disciple-making. By that we mean that you have to have faithful teaching in order to make a disciple, but teaching alone is unlikely to produce a disciple on its own. Why?

For one reason, there's only so much you can accomplish in a teaching venue. Time is limited. The average sermon is around 40 minutes, and you may get an additional hour or two from someone in a Sunday school class or small group. Couple that with the fact that many church members miss church regularly, and there is not much formal time spent under skilled instruction in the church.

For another reason, formal teaching venues are limited, and most leaders don't perceive themselves to be gifted or qualified to preach a sermon or teach a class. Therefore, church members are tempted to leave the work of disciple-making to the presumed experts who are thought to be capable of commanding a room.

Also, it's easy to be a hypocrite if all we have is teaching. If we fail to integrate our teaching with our lives, then it can be easy for younger generations to reject the very doctrine they once heard us espouse. An over-dependence on classroom style teaching can create distance between the teacher and the student so that it becomes difficult to actually model one's life after the older man or woman. For example, on average, a good presenter might use one or two personal illustrations in the course of a 30-minute talk. While these illustrations provide insight into the person's life, they are curated to make a point in the teaching. Those in the class hear an example, but it's far better to see an example in person. Teaching is necessary but not sufficient and the same goes for godly living.

WING #2: GODLY LIVES

Now think about the opposite. What if an older man or older woman merely seeks to make disciples on the basis of his or her life without any faithful teaching? Just like attempts to make disciples using only teaching, if we rely only on our good example through godly living, we will also crash.

Our oldest daughter plays the piano. I (Matt) on the other hand, do not have a musical bone in my body. What might happen if my daughter simply asked me to observe her while she plays? I might have enough rudimentary knowledge of how a piano works, but beyond that I'd be lost. Perhaps if I stared at her playing every day for an extended period of time, then I could pick up enough patterns to make some basic sense of what was happening. But if she were trying to train me to play the piano, it would be insufficient to understand only some of what she was doing and then sit down to try to replicate her skill. In order to help me, I'd need her to show me and tell me what was going on. She could use her playing as a demonstration of the truth that she was teaching, but her skill alone would be insufficient to make me a pianist.

The same is true in discipling others in the way of Jesus. We can live godly lives in front of them for years, and even if they have some basic knowledge of Christian doctrine, someone would need to put words to their actions for any of it to make sense or result in genuine life change. Our words bring clarity to our actions. If all we have is a godly life—as good as that is—we fail to teach subsequent generations to understand how the truth of the gospel makes those lives possible.

ALL THE TIME

We've established that you need faithful teaching and godly lives to make a disciple, which is exactly what the Apostle Paul commends in verse 7. He tells these older men (and infers the same for older women) that they are to serve as examples. The word "example" can also be translated as "mold" or "pattern." Examples are fixed forms that others can copy.

I (Matt) have learned to enjoy woodwork. I'm still not great at it, but the act of building a table or bookcase is fulfilling. There wasn't anything but a pile of wood, but hours later, the furniture is complete and people can use it, sit around it, or enjoy the craftsmanship involved. One day I'd love to take some woodworking classes to develop real skill. Most often I just see something that's interesting to me, study its design, take a few pictures, and then go home and try to reproduce whatever caught my attention. I then watch a Youtube video where an expert provides a step-by-step tutorial. With a little effort on my part and a lot of miscut lumber, I follow the example and make something decent.

Paul says the same about younger men and women. What they need most are older saints who will serve as examples of the change brought by the gospel of Jesus Christ. Paul then links a virtue with each—conduct your godly lives with integrity and teach with dignity. In other words, saints must take seriously the work of being an example. This work isn't a switch that you turn on for one or two hours a week. You've got to see all of your life as grounds for disciple-making.

Which brings us to a big idea—the best time to make disciples is any time. Teaching does not require a pulpit or a classroom. You can impart biblical truth to another person whenever you want. And the example of godly lives actually necessitates proximity. People need to see older saints living out the gospel on a random Tuesday afternoon or a lazy Saturday morning. They need to hear older believers connect the dots of how the gospel shapes their lives. They don't merely need a TED talk on the gospel, they need a tutorial on what gospel-saturated lives actually look like.

Think back to the famous passage from Deuteronomy that we considered in the Introduction. Here it is again if you've forgotten:

> Listen, Israel: The LORD our God, the LORD is one. Love the LORD your God with all your heart, with all your soul, and with all your strength. These words that I am giving you today are to be in your heart. Repeat them to your children. Talk about them when you sit in your house and when you walk along the road, when you lie down and when you get up. Bind them as a sign on your hand and let them

be a symbol on your forehead. Write
them on the doorposts of your house and
on your city gates (Deut. 6:4-9).

The command in the passage is to love God
and to help others do the same. Then the text progresses to ask and answer the "when" question.
When am I to go about this work? The answer: All
the time: when you sit in your house, when you
walk along the road, when you lie down, when you
get up. These words of life are so central to your
overall rhythm of life that you bind them to yourself, to your home, even to the city gates. Knowing
and speaking God's truth becomes a way of life, not
a once-in-a-while event.

There are two contexts worth emphasizing
here. First, the home. Parenting children is a work
of discipleship. With young children, parents instill
the words of Jesus daily through songs, Bible read-
ings, Scripture memorizations, and regular church
attendance. They faithfully instruct and enforce
clear boundaries, and discipline their children,
training them to obey the right authorities. As children grow into late adolescence and young adult-
hood, the role of the parent begins to shift to one of
influence as they help children reflect on their own

heart and the fruit it's producing. At this parenting stage, we want to train our children to apply the gospel to their own hearts. Many parents consider parenting young children to be taxing physically, while parenting older children is taxing mentally, emotionally, and spiritually. Godly parents gain influence in the lives of young adult children because these children observe how the gospel impacts the daily lives and hearts of their parents. But this influence can easily be derailed if we're not watching our own life and doctrine. The nature of life in a home is that we're constantly confronted with discipleship issues that must be taught and modeled. What will we, as parents, do with our sin—will we blame others, hide in shame, or will we confess and repent? How will we handle decisions—with our own logic, or with prayer and seeking the counsel of wise believers in our local church? Parents disciple their children as they model and teach their children how Christians live life in a broken world. Discipleship in the home is occurring at all times and the question we must grapple with is, "Am I using my influence to point my children to Jesus and away from other things they might be tempted to worship?"

In the same way, those in the church must also be about this work all of the time, and not merely when the church gathers. In their commentary on the Pastoral Epistles, Kent Hughes and Bryan Chapell explain: "God intends for the lives of the people in the church to interweave, to influence each other, and by these interactions, to testify to the truth, power, and hope of the gospel."[2] In a culture increasingly devoid of meaningful relationships, the church is to be a place where people necessarily intersect and interact in mutually beneficial ways.

Such interaction will require great diligence for older saints. You will not *drift* toward such intentionality. You'll have to invite others to meals at your house, to accompany you on trips, to participate in your favorite hobby. You'll need to be intentional about where you live, how you serve at your church, and how you'll be present in those places so that your life actually intersects with other Christians regularly. And when these lives do connect, you'll have to do more than fill the space with conversations about the weather, college football, or silly reels. You'll need to make it a priority to foster the types of meaningful conversations that allow you

---

2. R. Kent Hughes and Bryan Chapell, *1-2 Timothy and Titus: To Guard the Deposit* (Wheaton: Crossway, 2012), 355-56.

to commend what is true and to model the transformation that truth has brought to your life. As you do, you'll discover that most of the heavy-lifting of discipleship takes place as the church scatters throughout the week.[3]

Healthy disciple-makers use both faithful teaching and godly living to help others love and follow Jesus; and they do this, not as an event or activity, but as a way of life. This lifestyle allows ordinary Christians to have extraordinary impact on others.

---

3. Here I'm drawing on the distinction of the church gathered and the church scattered from Abraham Kuyper, *Rooted & Grounded: The Church as Organism and Institution* (Grand Rapids: Christian's Library Press, 2013).

CHAPTER 6

FROM DISTANT
TO DISCIPLE

"Your message is to be sound beyond reproach,
so that any opponent will be ashamed, because he
doesn't have anything bad to say about us."
Titus 2:8

Recently I (Matt) was traveling in Latin America for a conference. After one of my talks, a pastor in the region came up to me and said, "Can you tell me how churches grow in the U.S.?" Though we were talking through a translator, I understood the question. He was frustrated that his church didn't seem to be growing. When he looked at the highlight reel of the American church it seemed to him as if every church was bursting at the seams with new growth. He wanted to know how this was happening.

My answer was simple. Most churches grow through relationships. Of course, our church hosts various events and programs that seek to engage people far from God or far from the church, but for the most part, these activities do not lead to substantial change in those meaningfully invested in our church. People tend to connect with the church through relationships. And it's not just people who know the Lord or desire connection with the church. Even those who are far from God long for healthy relationships. If they find those with Christians, then these relationships can be a means God uses to draw people to faith in Christ.

NOTHING BAD TO SAY

Paul hints at the missionary force of a transformed life in verse 8 of our passage. At the end of verse 7 he linked the twin themes of faithful teaching and godly lives by calling the Cretan Christians to make themselves an example in good works and to teach with dignity (v. 7). He then continues in verse 8 saying that the message should be "sound beyond reproach." Here again, there is a key link. The word "sound" speaks of something that is healthy or whole, but the point here seems to be more than merely that the teaching is orthodox or right. The teaching is healthy and whole if it corresponds or produces the good works of worship that are fitting for God's people (Eph. 2:10).

When he writes that the teaching must be sound "beyond reproach," the Apostle Paul returns to a common theme. The most prominent time that idea has shown up in Paul's writing is in his qualification list for pastors when he writes: "If anyone aspires to be an overseer, he desires a noble work. An overseer, therefore, must be *above reproach…*" (1 Tim 3:1-2). The same idea shows up in the first chapter of Titus, though translators often use a synonym there: "The reason I left you in Crete was to set right what was left undone and, as I directed you, to appoint elders in every town. An elder must be *blameless…*" (Titus 1:5-6). What's important about both passages is that Paul goes on to list an assortment of virtues that are indicative of someone who is above reproach or blameless—not arrogant, not hot-tempered, not an excessive drinker, not a bully, not greedy, hospitable, good, sensible, righteous, holy, self-controlled (Titus 1:7-9). Therefore a person who is above reproach is defined by who they are which flows into what they do.

Paul's challenge to older men and women should be understood in this context. They are not merely to do good works or teach orthodox messages, but the truths of the gospel are meant to transform their character so that they live as an example with integrity and dignity (v. 7).

All of this leads us to the concluding thought in this section. If someone lives like this, then outsiders and opponents will be put to shame. Why? Because they don't have anything bad to say about genuinely transformed Christians (v. 8). There's a built-in assumption—those who do not love and follow Jesus will want to accuse Christians of wrongdoing.

We see this in our day. There's no accusation more easily lobbied against Christians than to call them hypocrites. Unfortunately, this charge is often substantiated, as professing Christians routinely undermine their credibility—often in profound ways. It's easy to see why moral failure would harm the reputation of Christ and the church. While Christians know that salvation does not immediately eradicate sin, non-Christians are taking their cues about who God is and what it means to love and follow Him by watching the lives of Christians. When professing believers cheat on their spouses, or get arrested for abuse, or are charged with financial misdeeds, or are simply snarly neighbors with a bad attitude, it does more than merely cause a non-Christian to not like that person. In many cases, the non-Christian then makes assumptions about the truthfulness of the gospel message based on what they observe. We think this is why Paul links dignity and integrity with sound teaching and good works. He wants to make it clear that a person can say all the right things and undermine his or her message with a sloppy life.

But what happens if the older man or woman is living with dignity and integrity? The outsider wants to accuse this person of being a hypocrite but can't (v. 8). They can't find anything bad to say. The Apostle Peter says much the same thing in his first letter:

> Dear friends, I urge you as strangers and exiles to abstain from sinful desires that wage war against the soul. Conduct yourselves honorably among the Gentiles, so that when they slander you as evildoers, they will observe your good works and will glorify God on the day he visits (1 Pet. 2:11-12).

I (Matt) was having a conversation with a friend who is a church planter in Pittsburgh. He's a good brother who's been laboring for four years in a tough place. The church is small but healthy. I asked him to tell me some of the ways he's seen God's faithfulness over the years and he said something to the effect of, "Well, our neighbors like us. The little community we are in seems glad that we are here. It's a highly secular place, so they'd probably hate my sermons or the doctrinal convictions of our church, but they seem to enjoy having us around. The community is better because the church is here."

This sentiment is a worthy goal for Christians in our neighborhoods, schools, businesses, gyms, restaurants, and community centers. We are called to live honorable, dignified lives filled with integrity so that those far from Christ but close to us see the change the gospel brings.

THAT DOESN'T GO FAR ENOUGH

At this point a perceptive reader could push back and say that it's not enough that outsiders simply don't have anything bad to say about us. We want people to love and follow Jesus. That's the goal. And, you'd be right.

Think about how we speak about the common work of evangelism and discipleship. Many times we use the word evangelism to refer to sharing the gospel with non-believers and use discipleship to speak of all that follows after they come to faith in Christ. However, Paul's challenge to the saints in Crete seemingly blurs these lines. After all, the younger men and women referenced throughout this section were once non-Christians. They've come to faith in Christ and are now given a means to help them grow in their new faith. This means there's a natural progression from evangelism to discipleship in the passage.

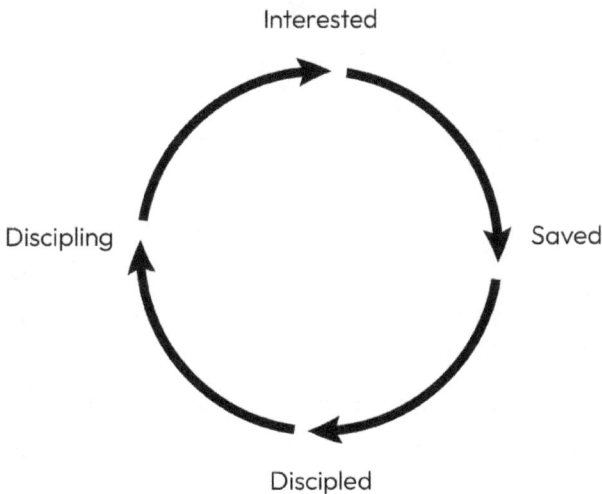

Interested

Discipling

Saved

Discipled

Let's think a bit more about the key link between people seeing the gospel lives of Christians and some coming to faith in Christ. Of course, there's no process that can mechanize the work of conversion. It is God's prerogative to save and He does so according to His grace and mercy (1 Cor. 3:6-9; Eph. 2:1-10). While we can't determine or predict how someone will come to Christ, we should consider how relationships are a tool God uses to draw people to Himself and move them to the place where they can be discipled. Let's focus our attention on how this might play out. Assuming that you are a Christian and you are seeking to obey the Great Commission to make disciples among the lost, consider how God uses you in the progression of someone drawn to the gospel.

Step 1: "I Have Nothing Bad to Say about You"

Non-Christians may come in contact with you as a believer, likely by virtue of where you live, go to school, work, or hang out. They see a distinctive pattern of life in you. Perhaps it's the way you talk, maybe the things you talk about, or what you choose not to talk about. Or it could be that they notice your hard work and integrity. They learn that you are a Christian, either because of your own testimony or simply by observing you read your Bible, pray, or talk about the Lord in a public setting. Because they do not know and love Jesus, non-believers are skeptical at best, hostile at worst (Rom. 1; Eph. 4:17-19). Therefore, they want to slander you as a Christian, but Christians who live authentically transformed lives give them no credible basis for accusation (Titus 2:8). At the start, this might be as far as you are able to get with someone. They simply don't have anything bad to say about you.

Step 2: "I'm Curious About You"

Over time, the relationship progresses. It may not always grow in depth, but if there's proximity with the lost for a prolonged period of time, then there is increasing opportunity for that person to grow curious about your faith. A distinctive life is compelling.

Sometimes curious people will actually ask questions. I remember being in the gym shortly after my dad died. Honestly, the gym was an escape for me. It was a quiet place where I could get lost in my own mind and forget about the difficulty I was experiencing. The gym was probably my favorite place in the month after his death for that very reason. But there were always other people around and many of them were people who I'd built a relationship with for years. They knew my dad had just died. Most of them said little, other than passing pats on the back and sentimental, *"I'm thinking of you"* comments. It's now been three years since dad's death, and in that time many other people in the gym have gone through really hard things. My public suffering as a Christian opened unexpected doors as months or years later those going through their own tragedy would start to ask me questions. What did I do? How did I cope? Where did I look for help? How did I find hope?

These types of questions seem to be at the heart of Peter's challenge:

> Who then will harm you if you are devoted to what is good? But even if you should suffer for righteousness, you are blessed. Do not fear them or be intimidated, but in your hearts regard Christ the Lord as holy, ready at any time to give a defense to anyone who asks you for a reason for the hope that is in you. Yet do this with gentleness and reverence, keeping a clear conscience, so that when you are accused, those who disparage your good conduct in Christ will be put to shame. For it is

better to suffer for doing good, if that
should be God's will, than for doing evil
(1 Pet. 3:13-17).

Non-Christians become curious when a Christian
suffers well. This makes sense because suffering is
universal and unique. It's universal in that everyone
suffers. Suffering provides a shared point of reference for all people. It's unique in that Christians
suffer differently. There is perhaps no easier place
to see the difference between a Christian and a
non-Christian than to observe what happens when
difficulty comes.

Since suffering is so crippling, it also makes
sense that people are desperate to find help and
hope so they are much more apt to want to discuss
faith. And it's those relationships where a Christian
has been faithful to live a life of integrity in front
of non-believers—even if they are unaware that the
non-Christian is watching—where these conversations are most likely to take place.

Step 3: "I Trust You"
When questions come, Christians can then give a
defense for their hope within these relationships.
The only way this works is if the non-Christian

trusts the Christian enough to allow him or her to speak truth, even when that truth is necessarily abrasive to the non-Christian. Once again, it is the good, long-standing gospel testimony of the Christian that invites this level of trust.

Christians speak on the basis of that trust. And they do so, as Peter commends, with gentleness and reverence. The main issue isn't that they formulate a 10-week class on the theology of suffering and invite the non-Christian to attend. Though this could be useful, what's most often going to happen is the type of on-the-go theology that the Chrisitan is able to integrate into normal conversation.

Again, take the gym as an example. You could see fit to invite a lost workout partner to a class being offered in your church. Perhaps a small percentage would attend. Or, you could drip theology into normal conversations as you warm up in the gym. These gospel nuggets could involve simple answers to questions like:

- Where was God when this bad thing happened?

- Does God care when we suffer?

- How does suffering remind us of sin and the need for a Savior?

- How was Jesus good news when you suffered?

The answers to these questions should come easily for Christians. Mature Christians may also be able to link their answers to these questions with Scripture to show that they are not merely inventing answers out of the air, but doing so on the basis of God's revealed word.

Here's how it might play out:

Non-Christian: "Hey, I'm curious, I know that you are a Christian, right? I know you went through some really tough stuff last year. Well, we just found out my wife has cancer and I'm pretty scared."

Christian: "I bet. I'm so sorry. You are right to feel scared and shaken when stuff like that happens."

Non-Christian: "When that happened to you, did you ever wonder if God really cared about you?"

Christian: "Yes. I think we all have big doubts when hard things happen. But once I stepped back from the immediate shock, I tried to process the news with what God says in the Bible. One of the things that I know is that this world is filled with brokenness and pain. I believe that's the result of sin—it's not all sin that I commit but it's the fact that our world is infested with sin and broken-ness. In spite of all that mess, though, I believe that God moved into the broken-ness of sin by sending Jesus to do some-thing about it. God did not stand off at a distance and wish that evil would go away, but He sent His Son to enter into our suffering in order to address sin and evil. When I go through hard things I'm actually given hope by the fact that pain and suffering will not have the final word because of Jesus."

Now this conversation isn't a mic-drop mo-ment and we're not implying that someone is go-ing to hear this testimony and immediately come to faith. But even as I type out those thoughts, this is something that I can actually hear myself saying to someone in a casual conversation. Littered in that little paragraph are gospel truths and Scripture paraphrase, like the reference to Jesus found in John's prologue (Jn. 1:1-14). It's a natural conversation that opens the door for further discussion.

Step 4: "I Want What You Have"

My experience suggests that people become Christians in all sorts of ways. For all, they come to faith by the grace of God (Jn. 3; Eph. 2:1-10). The process looks different for all. Some do so in a moment. Some in a church service. Some all alone. Some with a trusted friend. However the moment of conversion happens there's always been a process leading up to that point in time. There are those who will be able to see the providential path that God took them on to lead them to salvation. Others will only be able to see in the rearview mirror, often years after coming to faith.

Whatever the process, one thing is certain—relationships always play a part. We can't get too hung up on which person leads someone to faith. You might remember the challenges of disunity sprinkled throughout the Corinthians letters where people were wanting to pick their team based on their favorite leader. There in that context, Paul says: "What then is Apollos? What is Paul? They are servants through whom you believed, and each has the role the Lord has given. I planted, Apollos watered, but God gave the growth" (1 Cor. 3:5-6). In other words, any genuine fruit is attributed to the Lord and the Lord uses many people in many different ways to accomplish his purposes in a person's life. In almost every case, there are many people who play a role and often these people don't even know one another.

For example, take the fictitious Jose. He grew up in a Chrisitan home and often heard the gospel from his grandmother. He was resistant to the gospel and gave himself to prodigal living, but her words and her prayers were always ringing in his ears. Years later, he dated a girl who was a Chrisitan. She broke up with him because of his immoral life, but her witness and conviction to do what was right even when it hurt were compelling to Jose long after the relationship was over. After moving to the Northeast, he lived in a neighborhood where a small church plant met in a Boys and Girls Club. He never went, but he would walk past on Sunday mornings and catch himself eavesdropping on their singing. Months later, he was shocked to find out that his new co-worker was a faithful member of this church and a strong Christian. The day he got the news of his grandmother's death, Jose didn't have anyone else to talk to so he confided in this Christian co-worker and asked him to pray. The man did and continued to seek out ways to show love to Jose and testify to the gospel. The next year, this coworker invited Jose to an Easter service his church was holding and there Jose heard the good news clearly, placed his faith in Jesus, and was baptized later that month.

Humanly speaking, who led Jose to Jesus? There are two right answers. The first is "Who cares!" The work of evangelism isn't a ballgame, and we don't need to keep score. Jose is now in Christ and that's all that matters. The other right answer is "Everyone." All of those people—the grandmother, the girlfriend, the gathered church, the coworker, the pastor—they were all used by God to move Jose forward in his faith journey. Then, at a key point in time, Jose said, "I want what you all have. I believe!"

Step 5: "Can You Help Me Grow?"
Here's where we move seamlessly to the work of disciple-making. I like reserving the term discipleship for what we do after a person comes to faith in

Christ. I know there are those who would suggest that all people are disciples of something, so even when we invest in non-Christians we are hopefully pointing them toward being a disciple of Jesus—in essence, discipling them *to* Jesus and then, after conversation, discipling them *in* Jesus. The premise of that notion is fine, but it seems best to me to reserve discipleship for the work we do after someone repents and believes, is indwelt by the Spirit, and is truly a disciple of Jesus. In essence, discipleship is the outward work of the inward process of sanctification. Discipleship is the work called for in Titus 2:1-8.

The best person to disciple a new believer is someone who was instrumental in that person coming to faith in Jesus in the first place. There is already a built-in basis for trust in the relationship. The person has already seen something compelling in the other person's life. New Christians then seek to pattern their life after the older saint who played a role in them coming to faith.

We tend to hear that as an arrogant claim, as if the ones doing the discipling are boasting about their perfect life and inviting the younger person to become a replica of themselves. The Apostle Paul did not feel bashful about such a call. In 1 Corinthians 11:1 he commends the church: "Imitate me, as I also imitate Christ." It's the latter portion of this sentence that informs the first part. We are seeking to imitate Christ. We are making disciples, not of ourselves, but of Jesus. To the extent that our lives are lived by faith in Christ and in submission to His example, we can invite others to follow us as we follow Him.

It helps that this person presumably already knows you. Imagine the difference between taking a new convert and placing them with a total stranger in the church for discipleship right after they've been baptized versus inviting, someone they already know to walk alongside them. The former is better than nothing—far better to have a mature stranger walk with you in the early days of faith than to have no one. But wouldn't it be better if you had someone you already knew and trusted? This trust allows the call to "follow me as I follow Jesus" to feel warm and inviting, rather than brash and arrogant. The new Christian knows you and trusts you, so why wouldn't they want to follow you on the path to maturity?

There's one other way this link between evangelism and discipleship is helpful. Those who invest in others they've known for some time are also aware of patterns of sin that plagued their unregenerate life. Some might be prone to fear or anxiety or some form of addiction. Others might have an unhealthy relationship or immoral friend group. Knowing this information positions those seeking to disciple others in a great place to actually help.

Step 6: "Can You All Help Me Grow?"

There's one final step in the process, however. Yes, the main argument we are making in this book is that one-on-one, life-on-life discipleship from older saints to younger saints is the best way to promote Christian maturity; but that isn't to suggest that the work rests on an individual alone. We believe that God has given His Great Commission to the local church, not just to individual Christians.[1]

In the same way that we suggested that evangelism is a team sport, so too, is discipleship. God brings people to faith using many different influences and He matures people in faith using many different people as well.

---

[1]. This reality is implied in the link to baptism in the passage in Matthew 28:18-20, which suggests that those who come to faith are united to the church and taught to obey all that Christ commands in that context. Corporate disciple-making in the church is described as the process by which the first believers post-Pentacost were united to the church (Acts 2:42-47).

The new Christian, because of his or her existing relationship with a discipler through the local church, is then introduced to a whole network of human relationships that God uses to promote growth. Take Paul's classic mention of the body in 1 Corinthians 12 or Romans 12:3-8. We tend to organize these lists into spiritual gift inventories whereby a person can understand how they are gifted to serve the church. Often these gifts are then translated into areas of service that aid in the ministry of the church when it gathers—some people are greeters, some work with the kids, some lead music and so on. This isn't wrong, but it's not enough. What if we thought about deploying the gifts of the body in the work of discipleship? Someone's gift of mercy could aid in walking the new Christian through the trials that often follow leaving a life of sin to follow Jesus. Someone with a heart for service might come alongside this new believer to meet a tangible need. Someone with a teaching gift might be able to explain an element of theology that is difficult to understand. Seen in this way, the gifts of the body envelop new Christians and together, the church helps someone grow in faith.

Additionally, the gathered church plays a critical role. The person discipling the new Christian is not alone in the work. The gathered assembly of the church provides an abundance of grace gifts to help a new Christian grow. Faithful expository preaching, for example, helps the new Christian understand the Bible and understand how to read the Bible. It also provides fodder for meaningful conversations between the new Christian and the discipler throughout the week. Rich gospel singing helps to reinforce truths about the gospel that the new Christian is building his or her life on. The prayers that are prayed are enriching the spiritual life of the person and providing them with a model for how to pray. The informal greetings of the collective assembly reminds the new Christian of the joyful hope of the people of God. All of these are means of grace whereby a new Christian grows.

In the next chapter we will describe the path by which this person, in due time, can then progress to being one who can disciple others. But before we do, note the astonishing cycle that can take place when a person moves from being lost to being discipled to discipling others.

Take Pickleball. It's an odd sport to catch on, right? I remember the first time I heard the distinctive sound of the ball hitting the racket and watched middle-aged once-greats hobble around on a shrunken tennis court. I was oddly curious. At least they were active, I thought. Over time, my curiosity led me to the court. I certainly didn't have anything bad to say, and I thought, why not volley a time or two. All I could do was make the sport a bit cooler. I asked some people to explain the rules and played a quick game or two. My athletic prowess showed through, and it wasn't long before I ruled the court.[2] Now I wanted to identify as a Pickleballer! So what did I do? I let others who were better at the game show me the ropes. They did so by explaining the mechanics of the game, but more so by showing me how to play. The more I watched their play, the more I caught on to the game and the better I got. Not only was I a Pickleballer, but I was now being discipled in the game. But there was a catch. My skill placed a ceiling on how good I could get. I was a middle-aged wanna be, who, try as I might, could never be as good as my teenage children at the

---

2. Sarcasm intended, but emojis are not appropriate for formal writing so sarcasm is difficult to highlight.

game. I might be a Pickleball disciple, but I could never become a discipler.

Thankfully the line of demarcation between a disciple of Jesus and a discipler in the way of Jesus is not defined by skill. All you need is a bit of intentionality and a basic plan so that you and those in your church can move a person from one who is discipled to one discipling others. Let us show you how.

CHAPTER 7

FROM THEORY TO PRACTICE

I (Sarah) love IKEA.

I (Matt) hate IKEA.

I love IKEA because it offers a world of options. I simply follow the path and before me is every room imaginable. No need to actually buy the lamp or the chair when I can see what it might look like if I did. If I'm honest, I stink at decorating anyway and am easily paralyzed by indecision. So it's much easier for me to see what something might look like than to endlessly scroll online for a coffee table that I might end up hating once it's assembled.

I (Matt) hate IKEA because inevitably we do buy something. This means I get to haul an over-sized box to the house and open it to find some-where around 2,000 parts and a step-by-step instal-lation guide that rivals a Harry Potter novel in size. By the time I get to step 78 and find that I made an error back at step 3, I've determined that the $5 Swedish meatballs were not worth the 5 hours of my life that I'll never get back.

You've likely felt a similar frustration when it comes to disciple-making. As we said at the out-set, few Christians are going to push back at the stated premise of this book—all people should be investing in making disciples of Jesus Christ. But it can be difficult to put our intentions into practice. Much like IKEA furniture, we want the end prod-uct but aren't sure of the steps to take to get there and sometimes, if we aren't careful, we can make the work to get there so complicated that we lose heart and give up.

Our aim in this chapter is to help you think through a plan. We're honored that you've read our book, but that's honestly not the main outcome we've had in mind. Much more than simply read-ing thoughts on the subject of disciple-making, we want you to finish this book with a strategy to implement what you likely know you should be doing anyway—making disciples.

Let's organize our thoughts around this simple chart.

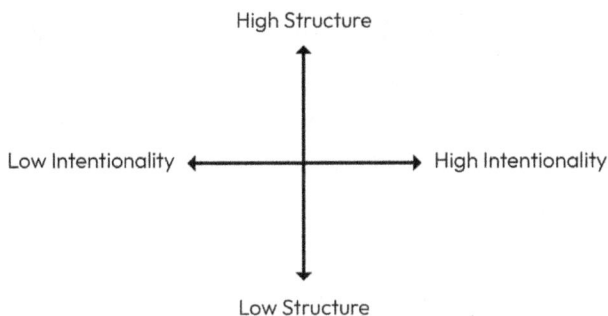

On the horizontal axis we have intentionality in disciple-making. On one end are those who are entirely passive—rather than seek out someone to disciple them or someone to disciple, they do nothing. On the other side are those who are intentional. They seek out someone and ask to be discipled or, as an older man or woman, they pursue someone to disciple.

On the vertical axis we have a scale of structure—referring to the level of formality and structure of the time the discipler and disciple spend together. On the bottom level are those relationships with no structure—they simply hang out, chat about whatever comes up, and do it again a few weeks later. The top of the scale represents highly structured relationships where there is a book or curriculum that they are working through together, an inductive-style Bible study, or a series of predetermined accountability questions.

Let's consider each quadrant in turn and show what can happen when you practice disciple-making this way.

LOW INTENTIONALITY
AND LOW STRUCTURE

First up, consider those who are passive and unstructured. To borrow language from the Apostle James, they know the good they should do but don't do it (Jam. 4:17). Maybe they are young Christians and really want someone to disciple them, but they just don't ever seek anyone out. When the church gathers, they are the last one in the parking lot and the first to leave. They hide in the shadows at church events or make small talk that never goes beyond surface-level facts.

Or maybe it's older Christians who feel guilty whenever someone talks about disciple-making because they know that's not a natural part of life. It's not lost on them that they are squandering these later years of maturity, but they can't seem to get up the nerve to pursue a younger person in their church. They are far more comfortable simply attending church activities and exchanging pleasantries with others than they are taking the risk to engage in meaningful relationships. What would a person think if I invited him to spend time with me? What if she doesn't like me? What if he sees my shortcomings and thinks I am a total hypocrite?

There are many parallels to the oddity of asking someone on a date—all of the "but what about" fears loom in your mind. But what if she doesn't like me? But what if it's super awkward? But what if I come on too strong? Many times young singles wait in silence for fear of what might happen. Applied to discipleship, passivity kills many mentorship relationships before they begin.

Passivity gets worse if we prefer low, or no, structure. Many times this desire for a lack of structure is at the heart of why we don't pursue the relationship in the first place. We don't have a plan of what we would do if someone agreed to discipleship, so we just never ask. We're often doubly paralyzed with fear if we don't know how to initiate

AND we don't know what we'd do if the person said yes. Maybe they'd just come over to the house or we'd meet at a coffee shop. We'd talk about life. Maybe something would come up that provided an in-road to a spiritual conversation. If so, then maybe we could discuss some Scripture that applied to that situation. All of those maybes are discipleship killers, especially for someone who's never done this before and feels insecure about taking a risk in the first place.[1]

We have a family of 7, so every meal is an adventure. I (Sarah) am not a big planner and I rarely look at the clock, so it's common for dinner time to roll around and I've not even thought about what I'm making. My lack of planning, combined with the various frustrations of the day, often create a harried time for me and my family. It's virtually impossible to walk into the kitchen at 6pm and have a solid meal by 7pm. But if I'm on my game, I have a plan. I've made a meal plan the week before. I've already purchased the ingredients for each meal. The meat is thawed and ready to cook. While

---

1. This danger is especially true for those who may be more introverted or who struggle with small talk. The thought of sitting around for 2 hours just chatting can give some people hives. I'll leave it to you to guess which of us fits this profile.

I still might not manage my time well, I'm much better prepared to make a quality meal and not get stressed out in the process if I enter the kitchen with the plan.

The same is true for disciple-making. If I'm going to do the work, I need both a clear intention to invest in a certain person and a plan for the time we will spend together. Without it, I'm simply going to be **negligent** in the task.

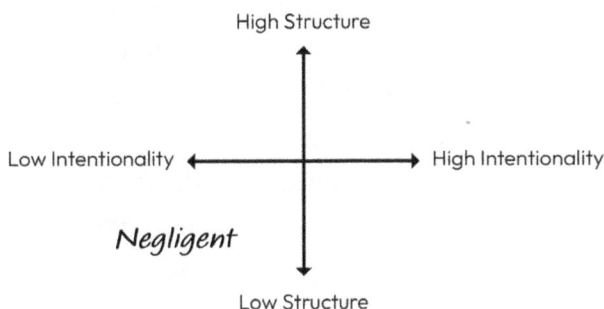

High Structure

Low Intentionality ←——————→ High Intentionality

Negligent

Low Structure

Low Structure + Low Intentionality = Negligent

LOW INTENTIONALITY AND HIGH STRUCTURE

Next, consider someone who is passive but prefers high structure. Here we have the same issues with passivity, either from the person who wants to be discipled or the one who can disciple. In contrast to the negligent person in the first quadrant, now we have a person who prefers a clear plan for the work.

Sometimes this preference is personality driven. There are those like me (Matt) who prefer a clear plan. We work best when there's a predetermined path to get things done. Calendars and spreadsheets are our friends. Our favorite day in class was when we got the syllabus and added all of the due dates to our calendar ahead of time. That was me, particularly as I got older and cared more about the subject I was studying. When the syllabus came out, I bought all of the books and read them ahead of the semester. Then, during the semester, I re-read the books I'd already finished in order to master the content. If an assignment was due at a certain point in the semester, I set a personal goal to finish the work two weeks ahead of time so I'd not be stressed with a looming deadline.[2]

This personality quirk has hindered my disciple-making through the years. I'm prone to want to map out a plan for a fictional relationship that's either too complicated or too formal for those in

---

[2.] And, yes, I also like to set my GPS when we leave for a long trip and race it throughout the trip to see if I can shave a few minutes off of my expected arrival time.

whom I could invest. I'm not the best at small talk, so sometimes I envision an odd interaction over cheeseburgers where I invite a younger man into my life and we sit around with nothing to talk about. Since I spend a good portion of my time in the academic world, I tend to want a scope and sequence for relationships ahead of time. Where are we going? What are we going to learn together? And how long is it going to take to get there?

Other times this preference is the result of what God has used in our lives. Sometimes people have seen significant maturity come through formal Bible studies, theological reading, Bible Study Fellowship (BSF) groups, or other structured environments. Since God used this form to grow us, we assume, surely that will be the same for others. So it's hard for us to imagine investing in disciple-making if it's not also rooted in some bigger program of our church or ministry.

These formal Bible studies or classes are highly structured and can serve a significant role in maturing younger believers, but they fall in the low intentionality category because the pursuit of maturity is still on the participant. The student is doing the work at home, possibly engaging in some discussion in the class, and listening to a teacher, but the environment is not always conducive to asking questions, providing accountability, or delving deeper into ideas. I (Sarah) have led many women's Bible studies and we prepare for attrition over an 8 or 10-week Bible study, knowing that it's easy to start with good intentions that diminish over time. In a formal setting like this, it can be difficult for a teacher or discussion leader to follow up with each participant to determine their maturity level or why their participation has waned. And, while the teacher or discussion leader may have great content, the size of the class means you're not likely to see how their application is lived out.

Those who lack intentionality and prefer highly structured relationships are likely to come across to others as distant. They may not intend to be intimidating, but it's easy to give off this sense to younger men or women who might otherwise love to spend time talking and learning from their example. Also, since those who live in this space tend to get lost in their heads, they may squander time creating the perfect playbook for a discipleship relationship rather than actually investing in the work.

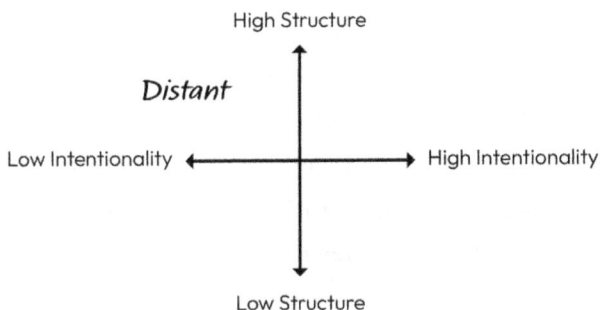

High Structure + Low Intentionality = Distant

This is also true for younger men and women. They may see older believers from whom they have much to learn but quickly find that this person lacks the type of structure that they may prefer. For them, simply getting together, hanging out, and talking lacks the intentionality they desire for a discipleship relationship so they give up.

HIGH INTENTIONALITY AND LOW STRUCTURE

Third, consider someone who is intentional and prefers low structure. The shift here is that those on the right hand side of the chart are willing to put themselves out there and invest. We'd say at the start that this side of the chart is far better. After all, it's better for your soul and your mission to at least try to invest in the work of disciple-making, even if you aren't great at it, than it is to do nothing. Intentionality beats passivity every time.

Here we have older men and women who see a church filled with younger saints and seek them out. They open their homes for hospitality. They are quick to offer to get coffee. Casual conversations with them easily morph into matters of spiritual consequence. This doesn't mean that these older men and women are all highly extroverted. It could mean that they are doing the hard work to put themselves out there in order to invest in others even if that work doesn't come naturally.

The same could be said of younger men and women who are intentional about discipleship. They are willing to have intentional conversations with older men and women in the church, even if they are a bit intimidated. Rather than surrounding themselves with others just like them, these younger men or women seek out older saints. They love to share a small group or Sunday school class with those much older. They know they have much to learn and aren't afraid to seek counsel, advice, and help.

Forming the relationship isn't the issue here. But structure, or a lack thereof, may be. There are two ways this shows up. First, because these people seek out relationships but don't have a clear plan for how to invest in the relationship, they can easily spread themselves too thin. Often these people are well-liked, so they are sought out for discipleship or they are the first people who come to mind when older saints think of who they can invest in. If they're not careful, the calendar can fill up with discipleship appointments and, rather than investing deeply with a few people, their energy is spread over dozens of relationships that lack real depth.

Also, if these people begin meeting together without a clear plan, it can be unclear how long they plan to continue meeting. Over years, this means that a person may still be meeting regularly with someone who they started meeting with years ago. Before long, a busy schedule will not allow any margin for them to invest in younger Christians who need it most—younger Christians who don't have a clear example to follow of what to do. This issue creates a bottleneck in a church's discipleship process where only a few people do the majority of the work of mentorship.

There's another issue with a lack of structure. We've already mentioned that some people prefer a plan. It could be their personality, their past, or even various issues they are facing at the moment. They want to grow in certain areas or consider certain subjects. For example, a widow may want to work through grief or discuss the theology of suffering and feel like these pressing issues are hard to bring up in casual conversation. Or someone may feel insecure about an area of her spiritual development, like Bible reading or prayer, but not know how to seek guidance when the small talk never drifts that way. Some may like a plan and sense that hanging out isn't the best use of time if they can't see clearly the purpose for the relationship or if they don't have a sense of how often or how long they are going to meet.

One's personality is not a matter of right or wrong and it may be that two people who both prefer a lack of structure seek each other out for discipleship and thrive in that environment. But it's more likely that the relationship will be confusing over time, and either the one doing the discipling or the one being discipled will simply drift away. In any case, relationships between those who are highly intentional with low structure will need to work diligently to keep the Word central to their conversation and to set expectations for the relationship that can help it to thrive.

High Structure

Low Intentionality ← → High Intentionality

Confusing

Low Structure

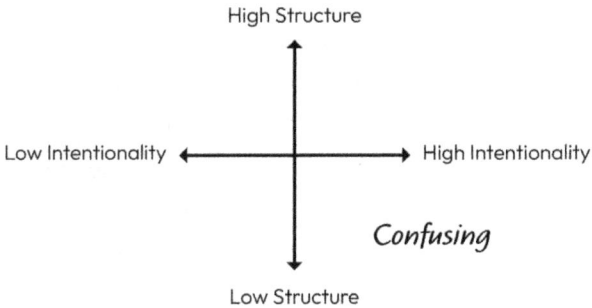

Low Structure + High Intentionality = Confusing

HIGH INTENTIONALITY AND HIGH STRUCTURE

Typically when someone walks through a quadrant model like this they end with the superior option. That's not the case with what we are suggesting here. We've said that anyone on the right side of the quadrant—those who are more intentional—are going to be more effective in disciple-making. But, neither highly unstructured or highly structured environments are necessarily superior. There is a huge upside to having a plan for disciple-making. Someone might have a set book of the Bible that they like to read and discuss. There may be supplementary books or curriculum that a person has used to help someone grow in the faith. Or, there might be a set series of questions that someone uses to hold another person accountable. Done well, a clear plan can help both the younger Christian and the older saint know what they are doing when they meet. It can take the pressure off of having to wing it each time. It can anchor the discussions in biblical truth, which may be especially helpful for someone who fears not being able to come up with relevant Scripture passages on the fly. A clear plan establishes how long the two people continue to meet and provides a natural transition to invest in a new person after the time is over. Finally, a good structure can provide the younger Christian with a tool that he or she can then use to disciple others over time.[3]

But there are drawbacks. Done poorly, this quadrant can feel **forced**. This is the area that I (Matt) would prefer, so the weaknesses are not theoretical but real for me and my work in trying to disciple others. For starters, a highly structured environment can be intimidating, especially if someone is coming in with little or no Bible knowledge and the one doing the discipling has walked with Jesus for a long time or has theological training. We are not able to know exactly what it's like to be on the other side of us, but we can imagine that the

---

3. See examples in the Resources section in Appendix 1.

new Chrisitan may feel pressure to prove themselves or live up to some standard they sense we have.

Another drawback occurs when highly structured relationships drift into the pattern where the discipler takes the role of a teacher far too often. In these cases, the discipler can tend to press to get through the content or make the theological points he or she wants to make without giving space for the younger Christian to engage or ask questions. Meetings can feel more like a classroom, and success can be measured in getting through the material or study rather than really focusing on the uniqueness of the person you are discipling. Those being discipled can easily feel like a project.

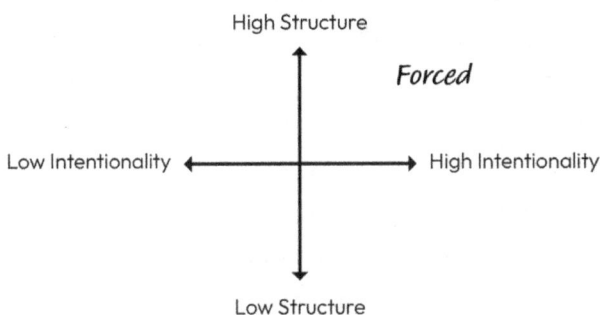

High Structure + High Intentionality = Forced

Another way high structure can feel forced is that we can miss the issues or concerns that are most in the mind of the person we are discipling. This isn't to suggest that there aren't times when we need to work through systematic content regardless of our circumstances, but discipleship relationships provide a context where we can focus on the areas of concern for the person we are discipling, while also suggesting some other matters of doctrine or practice they might want to consider.

For example, over the last year in our church we've had four couples lose children. Three of these children died prior to birth and one just a few short weeks after. Were you meeting with the parents of one of these children for discipleship, it would be unwise to simply work through your favorite discipleship resource at the start. The pressing pain is too great, so you'd want to start with some unstructured time to listen, pray, and apply God's truth to the grief they are feeling. Or imagine a scenario where you were working through J. I. Packer's, *Knowing God*, with a new believer and you got to a section discussing God's faithfulness, and the person you were discipling had all sorts of questions about eternal security and how someone might know they were truly saved. That week's session came and went; but the questions were still lingering, and you didn't have much time to provide sufficient answers. You'd be foolish to plow forward the next week and consider a completely new topic when the person you are meeting with needs to study God's faithfulness for several weeks in a row in order to really internalize biblical truth.

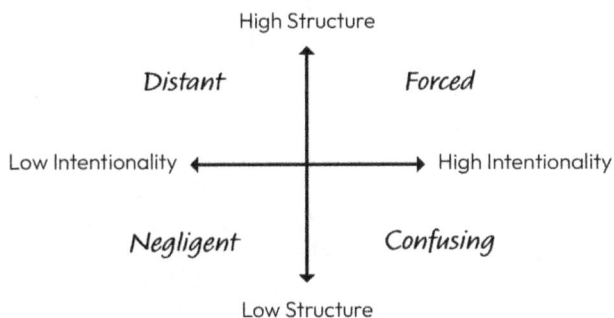

High Structure

Distant   *Forced*

Low Intentionality ←——————→ High Intentionality

Negligent   *Confusing*

Low Structure

A PREFERRED PATH

Were we to place the skilled discipler on this graph, we'd suggest that this person should be halfway on the right toward high intentionality. This stops short of all the way to the right where a person might be odd, overwhelming, or just too much for potential disciples. We want to be intentional, but not pushy.

And then a person who is midway along the structural line: by this we mean that we think it is best for potential disciplers to have a plan and some structure, but to be willing to modify that structure as you progress through the disciple-making journey.

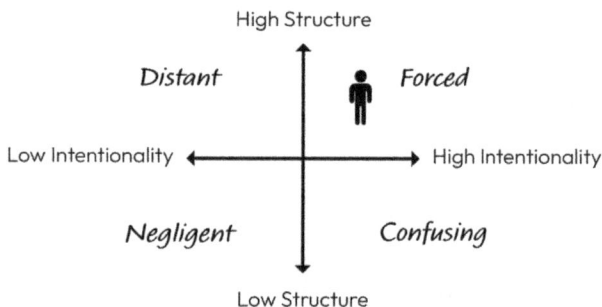

In this chapter we've attempted to describe two continuums that most people fall on when they seek to disciple others. As we've said, many factors influence where you find yourself on this chart. Like any good image, however, the point is simply that you have a visual representation of where you want to be and can take steps to get from where you are to that place. Not everyone will go about the work in the same way (and that's ok). What is important is that we all seek to be intentional about the process and have enough structure to support us in the work.

CHAPTER 8

FROM ONE
TO MANY

The hardest step is the first one. You've probably heard this cliché or one like it in reference to everything from running a marathon to overcoming an addiction. Like most clichés, the point is overstated but contains a degree of truth nonetheless.

A few years back I (Matt) ran a half marathon. By the time this book is published I hope to have finished another one. And, yes, I know, no one celebrates finishing a half of something. I should be a big boy and run a full marathon. Well, I can't! And I don't want to. Sometimes, half really is enough!

My handy computer just told me that a half marathon typically involves approximately 26,000 steps. If that's true, then I can readily admit that it wasn't merely the first step that was a problem, but virtually every step between 6,500 and 25,900. The first six thousand were fine and those last 100 were a joy, but everything else was pretty terrible. Nonetheless, the first step was the hardest.

I'm not a runner. By that, I mean that I am not great at running and that I don't enjoy running. My stride is all wrong, my feet are odd, and my lungs start to burn like my soul is leaving my body. The only reason I ran a half marathon (other than to be able to write about it years later and impress you) is because I like challenges. I feel like the human life is short and I want to push myself to do hard things as long as I can. So I tried. It was work to get me to the starting line. I didn't feel like a runner. I didn't want to show up. The race started at 5am. I get up at 5am, but I do so to greet a cup of coffee, not a workout. I had all sorts of excuses for not approaching the starting line that morning. But I showed up, in spite of my fears, and took the first step. And when I did, I took another, and before long I was running a race. And by the time I got to mile marker 4, I felt like I could push myself to get to mile marker 6. Then when I hit 6, I knew I could get to 8. Then by 8 I was over halfway there, so I kept running. And I finished.

There seems to be a strong parallel between my love/hate relationship with running and the work of disciple-making. We tend to psych ourselves out before we ever begin. Who am I? What business do I have investing in another person? What if it's a bust? What if he doesn't like me? What if she asks me questions that I don't know how to answer? What if it turns out that he is actually more mature than me?

These questions are normal, and anyone we've ever known who stepped into the work of discipleship has asked questions just like this. What separates those who give into fear and those who don't seems to be willingness to take the first step. You've got to actually give it a shot and take some steps, no matter how clumsy they might feel, in order to grow in confidence as a disciple-maker. And there's no better time to start than now. If you don't, you're going to read another book like this in five years or hear another sermon about discipleship and feel the same prick of conviction, except by that point you will have squandered five years that you could have invested in the work.

Our aim in this chapter is for you to finish this book and close it with great confidence that you actually have a path of obedience that you can take in this great work. So let's map out the path from the beginning.[1]

MARKER #1: SEEK

All discipleship starts here. Someone must take a risk and step into the relationship. It is a risk, no doubt. Any time we invite someone into a relationship with us, even if it's just for a short time, there's going to be some nerves required.

Older saints, this is where you can take some pressure off of younger Christians. Even though it's intimidating, an older Christian should be far more secure and fear failure far less than someone who is just embarking on the journey. You can ease the awkwardness by taking a risk to pursue a younger Christian in your church. Here are some easy ways to seek out someone to disciple:

---

1. David Helm's little book *One to One Bible Reading: A Simple Guide for Every Christian* (Matthias Media: Chicago, 2011) provides a plan for those seeking to meet with others to read the Bible. See chapters 4-6 for his brief outline of a process akin to one we expand upon in this chapter.

→ Pray. Ask God to show you someone and be attentive for what happens next.

→ Take note of who you sit near or serve with consistently on Sundays at church and use time before or after service to introduce yourself to them.

→ Leverage your church's discipleship strategy, whether it be small groups, Sunday school, or classes, to see who might be in your group. If these contexts are discussion-oriented, then it will be easy for you to hear people bring up themes that you might be able to address in informal conversation.

→ Ask your pastors for the names of some people who might be interested in discipleship. Good pastors will often know who is asking for someone to mentor them or who might need such investment. Also faithful pastors may be able to help pair you up with someone who has a similar personality or would be a good fit.

→ Watch the baptisimal. See who the church baptizes and seek them out. Each of these new believers could likely use someone to walk with them as they walk into their new life.

Wouldn't it be great if every person who was baptized in our churches had someone who invested in them for discipleship for at least the first year?

→ Ask your church's men's or women's ministry leader for help. These ministries can provide a great context to meet those who desire mentors.

→ Listen for prayer requests. As the church prays, listen for those who are going through difficulty and reach out to them directly. Even if they are already being discipled, they will be encouraged that you reached out.

→ Don't overlook circumstances. God is in charge of all things, including that random, seemingly chance encounter you had with someone in the hall or that church member who you just happened to meet at the playground with her kids. Pay attention to these little coincidences and consider that God might be bringing someone into your path.

Though I'd suggest that the onus of responsibility is on the older Christian, this doesn't mean the younger Christian does nothing but wait and hope. Younger Christians who want to be discipled should seek out environments with older saints. This may be as simple as changing where they sit on Sundays so they are around some older believers. Or it might mean joining another small group or Sunday school class comprised of older men and women. Events provide another chance—younger Christians can use conferences of the church to rub shoulders with different people. A prime place to look would be men's or women's ministry events, if those exist in your church. These contexts provide a great place to meet mature Christians and form a friendship with them that could lead to a more intentional discipleship relationship down the road.

MARKER #2: INITIATE

Once you have a sense of someone who might be a prospect for discipleship, we suggest that you initiate in two stages. First, simply ask them to connect one time. One meeting is far less awkward than inviting them into some longer-term commitment from the start. Just ask them if they'd like to get lunch sometime or come over after church to hang out or get coffee one morning. Something simple. Here's how it might sound: *"Hey, I've really enjoyed hearing you share some in our Bible study. I know that we don't know each other well, but it sounds like our stories might have a lot in common. I was wondering if you might like to have breakfast together one day in the next few weeks? I'd love to hear more about your story and share some of mine."*

Intimidating? Maybe. Odd? Not at all. Notice we simply took advantage of a point of contact we had with the person, made a general invitation with no strings attached, gave a long time window (next few weeks, not this week), and communicated a genuine interest in the person we wanted to get to know.

I (Sarah) jokingly advise not to begin the conversation with, "Will you disciple me?" This question typically comes to me from a doe-eyed college student on a Sunday morning after church while I'm trying to wrangle my family of seven so everyone is accounted for before leaving the building to get to lunch. This question can be intimidating to older saints and requires a definition of terms. My typical response to this question now is, "I'm so honored you would ask me! Let's get together for coffee sometime in the next week or two to talk through what that would look like. Send me some days and times that work for you." This doesn't commit me to formal weekly meetings, but it also doesn't shut the door on how the Lord might be at work. For the person desiring discipleship, a better approach than the question "Will you disciple me?" might be to ask "Can we get coffee sometime? Your prayer in our member's meeting was so vibrant and I'd love to ask some questions about how you cultivate your prayer life." Another idea would be to ask, "Do you have time to connect this month and let me ask you some questions about _____?" In essence you are asking, "Will you disciple me?" but these questions are less intimidating and still provide a chance for you to connect and see what happens.

MARKER #3: MEET

Pursue this first meet-up as a conversation between new friends. This isn't a presumably mature Christian finding a novice and forcing the person to come under his or her tutelage. This is just two Christian friends meeting to talk about what God is doing in their lives.

There are easy questions to get the conversation moving in a spiritual direction:

- How did you become a Christian?
- What brought you to our church?
- What do you see God doing in your life now?

- Where do you feel like you are growing and where are you stuck in your spiritual journey?

Of course, you will have to personalize these questions to the flow of the conversation and avoid asking a bunch of rapid fire questions, but the point is simply that you want to get someone talking. Thankfully, most people will talk about themselves. They may be introverted, and there will always be layers of their story that you will not uncover in the first meeting, but if you ask open-ended questions to explore the life story of another person, they will almost always give you something. You can take what they give by way of story, ask follow-up questions, and you'll be surprised at how quickly an hour or two will pass.

We do have a word of warning, particularly if you are the one initiating the time together. Since all people like talking about themselves, you are included. This means that it will be easy to spin the conversation to yourself and start telling stories of your own or making the interaction all about you. It's not wrong to share, especially if the person asks you questions. In fact, it would be odd to meet with someone and badger them with questions for a couple of hours and leave them feeling like they just had a polygraph test. But don't make the time about you. Share enough to be known, but keep the focus on the younger Christian you are seeking to disciple. Listen. Learn. Make some mental notes about them and, at minimum, you now have some intentional ways that you can pray for another person in your church.

Similarly, if this is a younger Christian asking an older believer for a first meet-up, come prepared with questions. Be ready to share what prompted you to desire hearing from an older saint. Be curious about their lives and listen as they talk for principles to apply godly wisdom and to practice obedience.

MARKER #4: ASK

Here's the point in the process where you are most likely to bail. Years ago in our early 30s, our family started a new church. To pursue that work, we had to raise a lot of money. For an entire summer, we set up meetings with families and friends and even some strangers to ask them to support us by giving to our church plant. Setting up a meeting took some energy, but it was easy. Getting there and having some casual conversation about life was no problem. Even describing the work of the church and why we were wanting to plant was fine. But then it came time to make the ask. There was a point in the conversation where I had to ask: Would you be willing to give a one-time or monthly financial contribution to this work? I always wanted to bail when it came time to make the ask.

When it comes to discipleship, the ask is critical. You have already made a series of asks up to this point, but they've been low-risk invitations. But now it comes time to ask to meet on a regular basis for more formal discipleship.

Before you ask, though, know that you should not ask everyone. The nature of this first meet-up is to give you time to discern if this might be a good fit for long-term investment. You might have a sense that the person isn't interested from the start. For example, it may have taken 5 weeks and 3 cancellations for you to even get lunch together, so you know that this person is either too busy or too flaky to commit to more regular meetings. Or, in the process for the first conversation, you might learn something about the person that you believe makes this a bad fit or makes someone else in your church a better fit to meet with this person. For example, you might hear a younger person talk about childhood abuse as he tells his story, and you were also abused as a child. The trauma is just too fresh and raw for you to engage, so you intentionally seek out another older person in your church to meet with this individual. There's no shame in saying that it's not a good match.

In most cases, however, there is no precise formula for an ideal match, and even if you don't sense overlap in your stories, you could have something to offer this younger Christian. You might sense that God was purposeful in arranging this meeting and see clear ways that your story, your life, and your wisdom could be used to help the person you are meeting with. So ask. Here's how it might sound:

> *"I've really enjoyed connecting today and hearing your story. Recently, the Lord has been challenging me to be more active in helping someone else walk with Jesus. I feel a bit intimidated by that, but I want to be faithful to what God is asking me to do. I think there might be some ways that I could help and encourage you and I know that meeting up more regularly would be good for my soul as well. Would you like to try to get together consistently this semester and read Scripture, pray, and talk about what God is doing in our lives?"*

Again, the exact wording is up to you, but the tone of this ask is what we are going for. Notice, the ask is personal. You are making yourself vulnerable to them by saying that you feel convinced from the Lord that this is something you need to do. This act of humility is a good place to start. Then you acknowledge that you are seeking to grow through the process. The ask isn't, "Hey, I'm a mature Christian, and you've got a lot to learn from me!" You make it clear that this relationship is intended to be mutually beneficial. This helps people feel less like a project. Next, the ask is dated, meaning it's not an open-ended, let's meet until Jesus comes back, type invitation. You ask them to meet with you for a few months. We suggest that you pick a time window that is long enough to provide time for the relationship to form, but short enough to give you both an out if it doesn't go well. The natural rhythm of life sets up well for this. Inviting people into an intentional relationship for the fall, the spring, or the summer seems like a nice window of time. Finally, in the ask, you suggest what you want to do. It's clear that you have a plan. We are going to read the Bible, pray, and talk about what God is showing us together. This shows the person that you've thought through the meetings, but that you don't intend to work through a rigid curriculum or massive book. As you listen, you may also hear a specific topic or area of needed growth that both of you could discuss during the semester. You could suggest a book or Bible study that addresses this topic for you to read and discuss together.

For example, recently I (Sarah) met with a younger woman from my church over breakfast. During our time, she expressed her struggle to understand how salvation happens, which led her to struggle to share the gospel with her children and others, and even to doubt her own salvation. We spent early mornings together every other week discussing a book on the doctrine of salvation to make sure she understood, and could articulate herself, God's work in salvation. She shared how this knowledge was impacting different relationships as she applied what she learned. The framework of a need—exploring a challenging area in her faith—provided direction for our conversation.

MARKER #5: ENGAGE

If the person agrees, then set a time and plan to meet. If possible, we would suggest that you map out a consistent time to meet rather than waiting until later. Since most people have fairly consistent schedules, pick a time when you are likely to be free each week. This is another rationale for having a defined period of time. You may know your schedule for one semester, but soccer practice or rehearsals or work may change from spring to fall, so pick a time period that allows you to have a general sense of your schedule. It might be every other week at 7AM for breakfast or a weekly afternoon while the kids nap. Set the time and try to stick to it, recognizing that there will always need to be last minute adjustments as life happens. We'd suggest that you set a time somewhere in the 60 to 90 minute range. This is enough time not to rush, but short enough that it can fit into the natural rhythms of life.

We think the easiest way to engage in the work is to agree on a book of the Bible that you will read together. This provides a simple roadmap for the time and helps to maintain the Word-centered nature of your conversations. If you've done a good job of mapping out the length of time you are meeting and the days and times of those meetings, then you know roughly how many times you will have together. Pick a book of the Bible that is small enough for you to break into that number of chunks and read through a section each time you are together.

I always start with the book of Ephesians. It's a book that is easy to split into 10-12 sections for reading and the book is dripping with gospel truth. And, since I've been using it as my starter book for discipleship for 20 years now, I have much of it memorized and I've learned ways to press the text into personal application. I would suggest that you do the same. I'm not necessarily suggesting that you use Ephesians, but pick a book and try to stay with it. The more you use it, the more it will be familiar and natural to you. It's much like your favorite dish to cook in or pillow to sleep on or shirt to wear—the book becomes comfortable.

Two other suggestions are worth mentioning. We have friends who like to use the Gospel of Mark for discipleship relationships. This seems to work especially well if you are meeting with someone who may or may not be a Christian. The Gospels keep the spotlight on Jesus from start to finish, and because they are narratives, it can be easy to read the stories and talk about who Jesus is and what He is doing. Since Mark is the shortest Gospel, it sets up well to read a chapter a week and you can fit most of it into a Fall or Spring semester of meetings. Finally, some like to use books like Proverbs or James, or even the Sermon on the Mount because of the highly practical nature of these texts. While I agree that these are seamless to apply, it can be easy to bend toward moralism or behaviorism and miss the gospel if you start there. That's why I like to use Ephesians first to develop a robust gospel foundation and then move to James or Proverbs for the next round of meetings to show how our obedience flows naturally from a right understanding of the gospel.[2]

There are three other approaches that I've seen work—though not as well as just reading the Bible together. Some use a series of accountability questions to guide the discussion. Every time they meet, they ask one another questions like: What is God teaching you from the Word? Who have you shared the gospel with? How's your prayer life? Are there known sins that you've committed? The aim is that these questions prompt meaningful conversations

---

2. Someone might ask - "What if I'm discipling someone who has been a church member for some time and is already familiar with books like Ephesians or Mark? Shouldn't I move on to something more challenging?" I say, "No!" First, simply because someone is familiar with the book doesn't mean that person understands it or knows how to apply it. Next, it's impossible to outgrow your need for gospel truth, so someone could not say that they've mastered a book like Ephesians and no longer need it. Finally, by using a book like Ephesians you are training this person on how to use it with others. So even if the person is well-versed in the content, considering it for the goal of discipling another person adds another layer of value.

and prayer. There are challenges with this model. For one, the questions require vulnerability in order for this approach to work. If the person answers in a simplistic manner, then the fruit of the conversation will be limited. Also, it's easy for the questions to become redundant and stale. Finally, this model requires that the discipler have the ability to integrate Scripture into whatever themes bubble up from the answers. Better, in my estimation, is to anchor the discussion in a passage of Scripture, and then use accountability questions that are clearly derived from the text. For example, if you are reading a passage of Scripture that presses the theme of evangelism, then it's wise to ask questions about someone's evangelistic fervor.

Others use the church's sermon series to guide the discussion. If the church is diligent to teach through books of the Bible, then this model can work well. The church's pastors have already broken a book into discrete units for discussion, and both the discipler and disciple have heard a sermon on the text, so there is ample fodder for discussion. One limitation I've seen with this model through the years is that people can spend more time discussing the sermon than they do the Bible itself. Once you've heard a sermon about a biblical passage, it can be difficult to re-engage the text with fresh eyes.

Finally, some pick a book to read together.[3] We like this model when applied to discipleship relationships that have some shared baseline of Christian maturity. When discipling someone who is new to the faith, it's almost always best to start with the Bible alone. But once someone has the foundations of the faith in place, it may be useful to add in extra-biblical resources that address a certain theme about which the person is curious. We've seen this work well when Christians are working through suffering and want a tool to help them think about God's presence and power in the midst of their pain, or someone who wants help with a broken marriage may find help by utilizing a proven resource on the subject. Whatever the case, it is essential to pick a robustly biblical resource or else this approach will benefit no one.

[3.] See Appendix 1 for a list of books we think work well as discipleship resources. Of course, there are more, but these books seem to be: 1) short enough that you could work through them in a semester, 2) accessible enough that they are not overwhelming for younger Christians, 3) practical enough that there would be clear ways to challenge one another to do something with what you've read.

We'd suggest that you prioritize books that make it easy to assign some homework or pre-work. Unfortunately, reading is often a passive act since we are able to stream books and listen to them while doing other tasks. If we want people to engage in the process of discipleship, they are going to need more than a cursory brush with good content. They need to consider what's being written and engage with how those themes apply to their world. Of course, a good discipler can ask insightful questions, but it will be better if the book itself has questions at the end of chapters or throughout the writing that force the person to slow down and think about the content along the way.[4] This level of engagement will provide a much richer discipleship discussion than simply if the person has half-listened to a chapter from a book while washing dishes or driving home from work.

---

4. This goal is the main reason I wrote volumes 1 and 2 of *Aspire: Transformed by the Gospel* (Timmonsville: Seed, 2016). The book is written like a journal, with sections of content followed by a question or two that is meant to engage the reader and allow that person to journal thoughts. In an ideal world, the person being discipled works through a chapter of Aspire while jotting down notes and then the pair meets to talk about the content and that person's answers to the questions found in the book.

Whatever you do, the key is to press people to the Word. You want to train people to seek God's help through His Word and not depend on you for all of the answers. This motive is a main reason we developed the Seven Arrows model for Bible reading (included as Appendix 2).[5] The arrows are simply an attempt to help people think about a natural progression to understand the Word, get to the author's intent, and apply the passage to life. In our estimation, tools like this help to guide conversation. I like the Arrows, or a close approximation to them, because you are asking the same questions about each passage. You aren't simply left to read a passage and say, "So what did you get out of that?" Nor are you depending on a list of study questions that vary from passage to passage. You can have the Arrows in mind, use those questions to talk through the passage of Scripture, and pray together at the end.

MARKER #6: DIVERSIFY

Simply meeting 8-10 times over the course of a semester is great, and you'll likely see fruit from this

---

5. Matt Rogers and Donny Mathis, *Seven Arrows: Aiming Bible Readers in the Right Direction* (Nashville: Rainer Publishing, 2017). I've included a copy of the Seven Arrows questions in Appendix 2 for those who'd like a tool to use for these discipleship relationships.

investment alone. But remember back in our passage from Titus 2 that we are called to serve as an example for others. This means you are likely going to need to diversify the ways and times that you meet in order for this process to feel more like true life-on-life investment than merely a two-person Bible study.

There are various ways you can do this. Sarah is a pro at inviting ladies over for discipleship during the natural rhythms of the day. She might have a young lady at the house helping her slice vegetables for dinner while they talk. Or she might take the kids to a local park and invite a young mom and her kids along so she can talk with the mom while also modeling how she parents our children. We've often had people we're discipling around our dinner table so they can see our marriage and interact with us as a couple. When possible, it's also great to find a time or two for more extended interaction. This could mean taking a day to go on a hike or play at the lake or go to a ballgame. It could mean a weekend getaway as families. It might be a night playing board games or Pickleball. While these more casual hangouts may not feel like discipleship, they build trust and allow for modeling far better than what can happen in one hour at a coffee shop. The main message we want you to hear is that you do not need to feel the weight of having to come up with something else to add to your calendar! Simply invite someone that you are investing in along to an event or activity that you were going to do anyway. You'll be amazed at how much you can accomplish if you take the same buckets of time that you are already filling with various activities and add some other people into that mix.

MARKER #7: APPLY

As the meetings progress, you will have an increased ability to apply the truth of the Scripture to the unique lives of the person with whom you are meeting. This is a place where life-on-life discipleship provides an opportunity that a classroom cannot provide. Often, if you are teaching to a group, you are left to take general themes of application and point out how your hearers might make application. But in a one-on-one meeting with someone, application can be much more specific. While you can't play the role of God's Spirit, you can intentionally ask questions or make points that are relevant to the other person because you know his or her struggles.

For example, you might be reading the Sermon on the Mount and come to the portion where Jesus says: [S]eek first the kingdom of God and his righteousness, and all these things will be provided for you. Therefore don't worry about tomorrow, because tomorrow will worry about itself. Each day has enough trouble of its own" (Matt. 6:33-34). Were you preaching or teaching this passage, you could mention a number of common ways that people might be tempted to worry. On the other hand, as you're meeting regularly with someone, you know exactly how he or she is prone to worry. You know the issues that weigh heavily. You know patterns of fear that tend to lead this person down the road of worry. You know exactly where he or she needs to be challenged to seek God's kingdom first.

Applying the Bible in the context of relationships is a bit of an acquired skill. The more you do it, the better you will get. You certainly don't want to be the person who goes into these meetings with a long to-do list for the other person or speak in edicts and demands. However, you also don't want to be a passive therapist who merely sits back and takes notes as the other person self-diagnoses his or her issues. Worse still, avoid being the person who only identifies and validates the difficulties of life without also pointing the person to the truths and promises of God. Practice is needed to learn to ask good questions and guide a person toward truth and application, and much of this practice happens as you do this work in your own life.

Again, there's much overlap in discipleship and the task of parenting, particularly as your kids age. A good parent isn't always telling the teenager what to do. The parent is working to gain access to the heart of the child, to ask good questions, and to steer him or her in the right direction, while also giving the child room to wrestle with hard questions or struggles. The best learning occurs not through telling, but through wrestling with the truths for themselves. Those who do this well are able to guide the child to the right conclusion, while making the act of arriving at that destination something of a shared endeavor. The children are much more apt to act if they believe they found the solution than they are if they are simply given commands to obey.

So it is with disciple-making. We want people to see how the Bible presses them to action according to the Spirit's guidance through His Word. In many ways, we as the discipler are acting as a travel guide along the path of obedience. The more they walk along this path with us as the guide, the less they will actually need us, and the more they will be able and willing to follow the path themselves and act as a travel guide for someone else.

One easily neglected but highly valuable component of discipleship comes outside of the scheduled meetings. There is tremendous value in sending someone a text message to start the week letting that person know you are praying about something specific that was shared during a discipleship meeting. You might also pass the person at church and ask about an area of obedience. These informal efforts to make application can go a long way to remind the person of what you've talked about in your meetings and to keep the issue before the person throughout the week.

MARKER #8: CHALLENGE

As the agreed-upon time nears completion, you have three routes. Route 1 is the least likely. You might agree that it's not best for you to continue to meet together because it's a bad fit. I say this is least likely because you've been meeting together for a number of months at this point. Most people who discern the pairing is not a good fit for whatever reason will stop before then. But, it may happen that you are faithful to finish the time and sense that your pairing isn't best due to schedules or stage of life or a perceived mismatch in the relationship.

We'd give one caution before you choose this route. Remember that disciple-making is a long process; you are not likely to see huge movement in a short period of time. You will be tempted to get to the end of three months of regular meetings and wonder if anything of substance actually happened. We'd encourage you not to measure success by what you can see or your perception of what may or may not be happening. Unless there's a clear reason to break off the relationship, we'd suggest one of the other two routes.

Route 2 is to suggest that you meet again for another semester or block of time. This route is almost always the preferred path if you are discipling a new Christian. You simply aren't going to be able to do all that you'd like to do in a semester. Now that you have the relationship in place and some good rhythms for meetings, why not continue? You may need to shift the day or time that you meet or adjust how frequently you meet. We've also seen people shift the style of meeting in the second iteration. Maybe they did a smaller book of the Bible or one that was a little easier to read and apply, and now they want to tackle a book like Romans.

Or, maybe they started by reading Ephesians and used the Arrows to discuss the passage, but the topic of marriage was particularly sticky when you got to chapter 5, so you want to use the second round of meetings to read a book on marriage and talk through gender roles. Once again, we would encourage you to make a time-bound commitment and not set up a sense that you are going to continue meeting forever because ideally you want to move all discipleship relationships to route 3.

Route 3 is to challenge the person you are discipling to do the same for someone else. This process is how the multiplication effect of the Great Commission begins to advance. The disciple becomes the discipler. This does not mean that the relationship with the original discipler has to end, however. We've seen it continue in two ways. Sometimes, especially if the person has never tried their hand at meeting with someone else, they prefer to continue in the existing discipleship relationship while also starting the process of meeting with someone else. This plan works especially well for younger adults, like college students who may have the time to maintain several discipleship relationships at the same time. The benefit here is that they now have a built-in relationship to draw wisdom from as they seek to invest in someone else. So as problems or questions arise it's easy to know where to go for answers. We've also seen this happen when the original pair spaces out their meetings so they are less frequent. For example, the person might now start to meet with a younger person for discipleship weekly, while agreeing to meet with their original discipler once a month.

Either way, the first discipleship relationship provides a springboard into long-term faithfulness in the work of disciple-making. The traveler becomes the travel guide and gives his or her life to raising up more travel guides who lead others along the path of Christian faithfulness.

CONCLUSION

This might be the last book we write together.[1] Ask Sarah about "our book" and she may comment about her aspirations for how the process of co-authoring a book would go versus how it really went. She wanted long date-days at the coffee shop with lattes topped with froth. She expected me to write a sentence and ask her to make it better, and for us to spend hours finding synonyms that make each paragraph sing like a Fredrik Backman novel. Had the process played out as Sarah envisioned, this

---

1. No need to text or write with concerns about our marriage. We are good.

book would be published in 2038, about the time we both entered a retirement home.

Hanging in our study is a sign with a quote from Walt Disney: "Get a good idea and stay with it. Dog it, and work at it until it's done right." Sarah gave this to me because she says it's the way I approach life. And, to her point, it's the way I approached this book, much to her chagrin. Our mismatched styles of writing are a microcosm of the different ways we approach pretty much every facet of life.

You'll need a bit of both instincts if you want to give your life to the work of making disciples. You'll need a plan and a strategy for how you go about the work. You won't be able to just sit back and wait for someone to come to you or for a spiritual conversation to materialize out of thin air. We've tried to give you a path to walk in this book but we can't push you down the path. You'll have to "stay with it. Dog it, and work at it…"

But to do it well, you'll need far more than a good plan. You'll also need genuine relationships. You can't make disciples if you don't love people. All the Bible knowledge and theory in the world will not get you there. It might not involve coffee shops with overpriced lattes, but discipleship will take time to cultivate real relationships.

The investment and cost of drawing solo, scattered people into the family of God will be worth it. When spiritual parents live out and pass on sound doctrine to the next generation, Paul tells Titus that they "adorn the teaching of God our Savior in everything" (Titus 2:10). We demonstrate that the gospel we proclaim is true because God our Savior changes lives and adopts diverse people into a family united by the blood of Christ.

Put these together—a clear plan, genuine love, and this worthy goal—and you've got a path for disciple-making that you can continue walking until Jesus returns.

DISCIPLESHIP
RESOURCES

We've chosen these resources because they are: 1) short enough that you could work through them in a semester, 2) accessible enough that they are not overwhelming for younger Christians, and 3) practical enough that there would be clear ways to challenge one another to do something with what you've read. There are hundreds of other books that could be used, but these seem to be among the best. We'd encourage you to consider asking one of your pastors to provide you with book recommendations or to review a book you think you might use for discipleship. As we said, books can be great, but they can also be terrible, so you want to make sure you pick one that's going to serve you well. These books are not necessarily about the work of disciple-making but are helpful for discipleship pairs to read and discuss together.

Jerry Bridges, *The Pursuit of Holiness* (Colorado Springs: NavPress, 2016).

Nancy Guthrie, *Even Better Than Eden: Nine Ways the Bible's Story Changes*

Everything about Your Story (Wheaton: Crossway, 2018).

The Good Portion series. (Fearn: Christian Focus Publications, 2018-2022).

Timothy Keller, *Counterfeit Gods: The Empty Promises of Money, Sex, and Power and the Only Hope that Matters* (Dutton: Penguin, 2009).

C.S. Lewis, *Mere Christianity* (New York: Simon and Schuster, 1980).

Timothy Lane and Paul David Tripp, *How People Change* (Greensboro: New Growth Press, 2006)

Paul Miller, *A Praying Life: Connecting with God in a Distracting World* (Colorado Springs: NavPress, 2016).

Ray Ortlund, *The Gospel: How the Church Portrays the Beauty of Christ* (Wheaton: Crossway, 2014).

J. I. Packer, *Knowing God* (Downers Grove: Inter-Varsity Press, 1973).

Micheal Reeves, *Delighting in the Trinity: An Introduction to the Christian Faith* (Downers Grove: InterVarsity Press, 2012).

Matt Rogers, *Aspire: Transformed by the Gospel* (Timmonsville: Seed Publishers, 2016).

A. W. Tozer, *The Knowledge of the Holy: The Attributes of God: Their Meaning for the Christian Life* (San Francisco: HarperOne, 2009).

Mark Vroegop, *Dark Clouds, Deep Mercy: Discovering the Grace of Lament* (Wheaton: Crossway, 2019).

Ed Welch, *When People are Big and God is Small: Overcoming Peer Pressure, Codependency, and the Fear of Man* (Phillipsburg: P&R Publishing, 1997).

Many years back I doodled a few arrows on a dinner napkin to try to help a young man I was discipling read the Bible well. Over the years these arrows have proven far more useful than I expected at the time. This tool, or another simple method for Bible reading, can be a wonderful help when you are seeking to work through a book of the Bible with someone whom you are discipling.

7 ARROWS OF BIBLE READING *Donny Mathis & Matt Rogers*	What does this passage tell us about man?
What does this passage say?	What does this passage demand of me?
What did this passage mean to its original audience?	How does this passage change the way I relate to people?
What does this passage tell us about God?	What does this passage prompt me to pray to God?